Praise for Jonathan Lethem's

The Disappointment Artist

"Brilliant. . . . Part literary criticism, part film analysis and wholly memoir, it is a hybrid tour de force that engages simultaneously mind and heart. . . . Takes the memoir form to the highest level with breathtaking honesty." —*Chicago Tribune*

"To read Jonathan Lethem is to come away inspired. . . . Lethem writes so passionately and personally about books and records and paintings and architecture that he makes you want to be a better reader, listener and viewer. . . . There's something quotable on every page. . . . These essays are Lethem's great song." —*Newsday*

"Transcendent and gorgeous." —*Nerve.com*

"Engaging. . . . Arresting and meaningful. . . . These are the highest form of personal culture essays: They explain what the subject means to the writer and then, through the use of story, they chart how that meaning became a strand in the dirty rubber-band ball he calls his self." —*San Francisco Chronicle*

"Intelligent. . . . Reveals the artistic and personal forces that shaped one of America's most innovative novelists." —*The Miami Herald*

"Like a good fisherman, Lethem is trolling deeper waters, seeking out leviathans of the sort that haunt and obsess us all our lives. . . . A revealing glimpse into the soul of one of America's most interesting young writers."   —*The Denver Post*

"These essays give as poignant a sense of Jonathan Lethem's adolescence as any more concerted assault on the project of writing a memoir."
—*The Boston Globe*

"Compelling. . . . Sweetly self-conscious. . . . [The] essay devoted to the Western *The Searchers* does a great job of demystifying movie-geek compulsiveness. Lethem's love letter to comic books, 'Identifying with Your Parents,' could convey even to the most graphically illiterate the importance of the old-school artist Jack Kirby."   —*New York Post*

"Lethem's trademark pop insight makes this slim volume a remarkable read."   —*Entertainment Weekly*

"Always fascinating, sometimes quite affecting and just as often laugh-out-loud funny . . . [with] a depth of observation, and personal confessional, that goes beyond what one normally expects in critical essays."
—*Sci Fi Magazine*

"Funny, frequently moving. . . . Evocative."   —*Time Out New York*

"Lethem proves to be a masterful essayist. . . . Witty, accessible and slightly self-mocking, his voice is that of a friend who's smarter than you, but who doesn't make you resent him for it. But there's also a moving emotional depth to *Artist*. . . . [An] impressive nonfiction debut."
—*Time Out Chicago*

"Exemplary. . . . Lethem [writes] with prickly originality and personal exhilaration."   —*The Buffalo News*

JONATHAN LETHEM

The Disappointment Artist

Jonathan Lethem is the author of six novels, including *The Fortress of Solitude* and *Motherless Brooklyn*, which won the National Book Critics Circle Award. He is also the author of two short story collections, *Men and Cartoons* and *The Wall of the Sky, The Wall of the Eye*, and the editor of *The Vintage Book of Amnesia*. His essays have appeared in *The New Yorker*, *Rolling Stone*, *Granta*, and *Harper's*. He lives in Brooklyn and Maine.

BOOKS BY JONATHAN LETHEM

The
Disappointment
Artist

AND OTHER ESSAYS

JONATHAN LETHEM

Vintage Contemporaries
Vintage Books
A Division of Random House, Inc.
New York

FIRST VINTAGE CONTEMPORARIES EDITION, MARCH 2006

Copyright © 2005 by Jonathan Lethem

All rights reserved. Published in the United States by Vintage Books, a division of Random House, Inc., New York, and in Canada by Random House of Canada Limited, Toronto. Originally published in hardcover in the United States by Doubleday, a division of Random House, Inc., New York, in 2005.

Vintage and colophon are registered trademarks and Vintage Contemporaries is a trademark of Random House, Inc.

Versions of some of these essays have appeared elsewhere: "Defending *The Searchers*" in *Tin House*; "The Disappointment Artist" in *Harper's*; "13, 1977, 21" in *The New Yorker* and in *A Galaxy Not So Far Away*; "Speak, Hoyt-Schermerhorn" in *Harper's*; "Indentifying with Your Parents" in *The London Review of Books* and *Give My Regards to the Atomsmashers!*; "You Don't Know Dick" in *Bookforum*; "Lives of the Bohemians" in *Modern Painters*; and "Two or Three Things I Dunno About Cassavetes" in *Granta* and in the Criterion Collection Cassavetes box set.

My thanks to the individual editors and in particular to Sean Howe, as well to David Shields, Laura Miller, Phillip Lopate, Zoë Rosenfeld, Kat Silverstein, David Hyde, Edward Kastenmeier, Richard Parks, and Bill Thomas.

The Library of Congress has cataloged the Doubleday edition as follows:
Lethem, Jonathan.
The disappointment artist and other essays / Jonathan Lethem.—1st ed.
p. cm.
I. Title.
PS3562.E8544D57 2005
814'.54—dc22
2004055133

Vintage ISBN-10: 1-4000-7681-1
Vintage ISBN-13: 978-1-4000-7681-9

Book design by Caroline Cunningham

www.vintagebooks.com

Printed in the United States of America
10   9   8   7   6   5   4   3   2

814.54
LET
2006

For Maureen Linker

Contents

Defending *The Searchers*

(Scenes in the Life of an Obsession)

1. Bennington

What's weird in retrospect is how I seem to have willed the circumstances into being, how much I seemed to know before I knew anything at all. There shouldn't have been anything at stake for me, seeing *The Searchers* that first time. Yet there was. Going to a film society screening was ordinarily a social act, but I made sure to go alone that night. I smoked a joint alone too, my usual preparation then for a Significant Moment. And I chose my heavy black-rimmed glasses, the ones I wore when I wanted to appear nerdishly remote and intense, as though to decorate my outer self with a confession of inner reality. The evening of that first viewing of *The Searchers* I readied myself like a man who suspects his first date might become an elopement.

I wasn't a man. I was nineteen, a freshman at Bennington, a famously expensive college in Vermont. I'd never been to private school, and the distance between my experience and the other students', most of whom had never set foot inside a public school like those I'd attended in Brooklyn, would be hard to overstate. On the surface I probably came off like an exuberant chameleon. I plied my new friends with stories of inner-city danger when I wanted to play the exotic, aped their precocious cynicism when I didn't. Beneath that surface I was weathering a brutally sudden confrontation with the reality of class. My bohemian-artisan upbringing—my parents were hippies—had masked the facts of my own exclusion from real privilege, more adeptly than is possible anymore. It was 1982.

Soon the weight of these confusions crushed my sense of belonging, and I dropped out. But before that, I cloaked my abreaction in a hectic show of confidence: I was the first freshman ever to run the film society. The role freed me to move easily through the complex social layers at Bennington, impressing people with a brightness that hadn't affixed to any real target. Plus I was able to hire myself as a projectionist, one of the least degrading work-study jobs, then pad the hours, since I was my own manager.

So when I walked into Tishman Hall, Bennington's small, free-standing movie theater, I was entering my own little domain on a campus that really wasn't mine at all. Which had everything to do with the episode that night. The rows of wooden seats in Tishman were full—deep in the Vermont woods, any movie was diversion enough for a Tuesday night—but I doubt any of my closest friends were there. I don't remember. I do remember glancing up at the booth to see that this night's projectionist was my least competent. The lights dimmed, the babble hushed, and the movie began.

A cowboy ballad in harmony plays over the titles. You're thrust into a melodrama in blazing Technicolor, which has faded to the color of worrisome salmon. A homestead on the open range—no, hardly the range. This family has settled on the desolate edge of Monument Valley, under the shadow of those baked and broken monoliths rendered trite by Jeep commercials. You think: they might as well try to farm on the moon. The relationships between the characters are uneasy, murky, despite broad performances, corny lines. At the center of the screen is this guy, a sort of baked and broken monolith himself, an actor you might feel you were supposed to know. John Wayne.

I'd seen part of *Rooster Cogburn* on television. The only feature Western I'd ever watched was *Blazing Saddles*, but I'd passingly absorbed the conventions from *F Troop*, from *Gunsmoke*, from a *Mad Magazine* parody of *3:10 to Yuma*. Similarly, I'd grasped a sense of John Wayne's iconographic gravity from the parodies and rejections that littered seventies culture. I knew him by his opposite: something of Wayne's force is encoded in Dustin Hoffman, Elliott Gould, Alan Alda. And the voice—in high school I'd sung along with a hit song called "Rappin' Duke" which aped his bullying drawl: "So you think you're bad, with your rap / Well I'll tell ya, Pilgrim, I started the crap—"

As for movies, I was a perverse muddle, another result of my parents' milieu. I'd seen dozens by Godard and Truffaut, and never one by Howard Hawks or John Ford. My parents had taken me to *The Harder They Come*, not *The Wizard of Oz*. In my scattershot reading I'd sensed something missing in my knowledge, something central, a body of Hollywood texts the European directors revered like a Bible. But I'd never seen an American film older than *Dr. Strangelove*. Somewhere in my reading I'd also gleaned that *The Searchers* was terribly important, though not how, or why, or to whom.

Wayne's character, Ethan, is tormented and tormenting. His fury is righteous and ugly—resentment worn as a fetish. It isolates him in every scene. It isolates him from you, watching, even as his charisma wrenches you closer, into an alliance, a response that's almost sexual. You try to fit him to your concept of hero, but though he's riding off now, chasing a band of murderous Indians, it doesn't work. No parody had prepared you for this. Wasn't Wayne supposed to be a joke? Weren't Westerns meant to be simple? The film on the screen is lush, portentous. You're worried for it.

Now Wayne and the other riders falter. The Indians, it seems, have circled back, to raid the farmhouse the riders have left behind. The family, they're the ones in danger. The riders race back in a panic. They've failed. The farmhouse is a smoldering cinder, the family dead. The woman Wayne seemed to care for, raped and murdered. Her daughter, Wayne's niece, kidnapped. The sky darkens. The score is a dirge, no ballad now. Wayne squints, sets his jaw: the girl would be better dead than in the hands of the savages. John Wayne's a fucking monster! So are the Indians!

Now you're worried in a different way.

That's when the audience in Tishman began laughing and catcalling. Some, of course, had been laughing from the start, at the conventions of 1950s Hollywood. Now, as the drama deepened and the stakes became clear, the whole audience joined them. It was the path of least resistance. The pressure of the film, its brazen ambiguity, was too much. It was easier to view it as a racist antique, a naïve and turgid artifact dredged out of our parents' bankrupt fifties culture.

Benefit of the doubt: What cue, what whiff of context was there to suggest to this audience why it should risk following where this film was going? These were jaded twenty-year-old sophisticates, whose idea of a film to ponder was something sultry and pretentious—*Liquid Sky, The Draughtsman's Contract*. If an older film stood a chance it should be in black-and-white, ideally starring Humphrey Bogart, whose cynical urbanity wouldn't appall a young crowd nursing its fragile sense of cool. The open, colorful manner of *The Searchers* didn't stand a chance. A white actor wearing dark makeup to play the main Indian character didn't stand a chance. John Wayne, above all, didn't stand a chance. The laughter drowned out the movie.

I was confused by the film, further confused by the laughter. *The Searchers* was overripe, and begged for rejection. But the story was beginning to reach me, speak to me in its hellish voice, though I didn't understand what it was saying. And I clung to shreds of received wisdom—this was the film that meant so much to . . . who was it? Scorsese? Bogdanovich? There must be something there. The laughter, I decided, was fatuous, easy. A retreat. Sitting there trying to watch through the howls, I boiled.

Then the film broke. The crowd groaned knowingly. This wasn't uncommon. The lights in the booth came up, illuminating the auditorium, as my projectionist frantically rethreaded the projector. It was then I began daring myself to speak, began cobbling together and rehearsing words to express my anger at the audience's refusal to give *The Searchers* a chance. A print brittle enough to break once in Tishman's rusty projectors was likely to do it again, and by the time the film was up and running I'd made a bargain with myself: if there was another break I'd rise and defend the film.

My silent vow scared the shit out of me. I sat trembling, hating the crowd, hating myself for caring, and praying the film wouldn't break again. *The Searchers* was meant to be the center of this experience, but with one thing and another it was reeling away from me.

It did break again. I did stand and speak. What I recall least about that night are the words which actually came out of my mouth, but you can bet they were incoherent. I'd love to claim I said something about how *presentational strategies that look natural to us in contemporary films would look just as silly to an audience in the future as those in* The Searchers *did to us now.* I'd love to think I said something about *an American tendency to underestimate the past,* that I planted a seed by suggesting *The Searchers* had been put together *by artists with a self-consciousness, possibly even a sense of irony, of their own.*

Of course, I didn't. I was nineteen. I called them idiots and told them to shut up. What I didn't do, couldn't do, was defend *The Searchers* itself. I hadn't seen more than a third of the film, after all, and what I'd seen I hadn't understood. My schoolmates might be wrong to condescend to this film, but I couldn't tell them why. Years later I'd come to see that part of what I was defending, by instinct, was the fact that the film had the lousy taste to be a Western in the first place. The aspiring novelist who'd soon make his first clumsy attempts to work out his surrealist impulses in the despised medium of science fiction felt kinship with John Ford, a director who persistently cast his moral sagas in the despised form of the genre Western. The indignation I felt was partly on my own behalf, indignation I couldn't express because I was ashamed of it. So *The Searchers* and I began our relationship with a grudge in common, but at that moment, under the astonished eyes of my schoolmates, I was only sure I'd made some irrevocable commitment, laid my cards on the table. I didn't know which cards, or what table.

I sat. The film started again. The audience was quieter, mainly because it had thinned. In the face of this unpromising night, this ludicrous film they'd now been informed they weren't allowed to laugh at, and who knew how many breakages to come, half the audience opted for the campus café, for an early corner on a booth and pitcher of beer. Face burning, I settled in for my hard-won film, determined now to see its greatness. But the worst was to come. For then *The Searchers* betrayed me. Fifteen minutes after my speech came a scene of such giddy misogyny, such willful racism, it seemed indefensible by design.

During a comic mix-up at an Indian barter session, Wayne's sidekick has inadvertently acquired an Indian wife. The sidekick and Wayne tolerate her presence, barely, until nightfall. When they bed down by the fire the chubby Indian girl slides in beside the sidekick, drawing exaggerated and unfunny derision from Wayne. The sidekick, enraged, kicks the girl out of his bedroll, so hard she cascades down a hill. There she ends in the dust, weeping, her ludicrous marriage in ruins. Wayne hoots with pleasure, his eyes maniacal. The scene is odious. The chance Wayne might be some kind of hero, that the filmmakers might redeem him, or themselves, has been pissed away.

The crowd bellowed, cawed. There were more defections. Those who stayed were ruthless, their suspicions confirmed, surpassed. *The Searchers* had slapped me down. I had to sit it out, of course, though now I was suspicious of the film, of the audience, of myself. My watching brain did worse than withdraw. It became autistic. After the turmoil of the first half, I followed the rest as a plot schematic, unable to risk any identification or strong response. *The Searchers* was only a camp opportunity after all. I was a fool.

2. San Francisco

D. was a junkie, though not at first. When we met, D. was one of the most dauntingly clever, well-read, and pop-culturally savvy people I'd known. He'd written for a legendary L.A. fanzine, was friends with a famous underground cartoonist and a famous punk singer. I was honored to be collected into this company. D. was also a sweet and devoted friend. Just a bit of a drinker, and with a weakness for speed, then overly fond of Ecstasy. I'd indulged with him at times—we went to see the first *Batman* movie together on mushrooms—but I could never keep up with him, never go the lengths.

When D. got involved with heroin he began pilfering from and lying to his friends, as though working by rote through some shopworn guidebook to junkie behavior. I avoided him, not systematically, but in guilt at his decline and my complicity. The pleasures in knowing D. had slowly evaporated anyway, mercurial charm replaced by boozy maunderings, devoted attentiveness by passive-aggressive gambits. Besides, I had to protect my stuff, my pawnable books and records. Our friendship became a room we'd both abandoned.

Then D. came to share a large apartment in San Francisco with three roommates, one of whom was my girlfriend. There I'd edge past him in the corridor and kitchen, exchange pleasantries, try not to get caught alone. His method-actorish comings and goings for "cigarettes," his jittery, sweaty jags, all were made awfully plain there. The three roommates and I were a microscope D. was under, and we took too much satisfaction from watching our sample squirm, nodding and rolling our eyes at one another to excuse our collective failure, the fact that we'd let someone rare and fragile plummet into depravity on our watch. It was a terrible place, and we were all locked into a terrible stasis.

One day I rented a videotape of *The Searchers* and brought it to the apartment. This was seven years after the screening at Bennington. I hadn't seen the film since, though I'd prepared plenty, read about it anywhere I could, gathered evidence of its greatness. I needed to justify being stirred that first time, to prove that the force of that moment was more than a neurotic projection, that it resided in the film, intrinsic. In the process, of course, I'd repeated my mistake: this second viewing was already overburdened. (In fact I was about to begin a novel I'd predetermined should be influenced by *The Searchers*.) Armed with cribbed defenses of various aspects of the film, I was ready to lecture my girlfriend as we watched: See, Wayne's the villain of the piece until the end; see, it's a film about racism, obsession, America; John Ford was made an honorary member of the tribe, you know—he actually *spoke* Navaho. She: Gosh! So went the fantasies. I was plotting to remake my scene in Tishman Hall, only this time the audience would be completely under my guiding hand. We would enter the temple of *The Searchers* together. Her awe would confirm and justify my own.

D. paced into the living room about ten minutes into the running of the video, and my heart sank. I hadn't known he was home. When he joined us I hastily, despairingly sketched the start of the film's plot to bring him up to speed. D. couldn't keep still, but between mysterious time-outs behind his bedroom door he gave the film what he could of his slipshod attention. I went back to watching as hard as I could, hell-bent on preserving the sacredness of the moment, feeding my girlfriend just as many interpretations as I thought she'd bear. We both pretended D. wasn't listening.

D. was smart enough to detect my near-hysterical reverence, and it irritated him. The veneer of civility between us was thin by then. Seizing an advantage, he began picking at the film.

"Come on, Jonathan. It's a Hollywood Western."

I wanted to reply that any film became generic if you reduced it to a series of disconnected scenes by flitting in and out of the room. Instead I bit my tongue.

"You're giving it too much credit."

What *The Searchers* requires is focus, patience, commitment, I thought. Things you're now incapable of giving.

"You don't really think John Ford was conscious—"

A thousand times more conscious than you, I thought. My heart was beating fast.

Then he burst out laughing. We'd come to the first battle scene, where Indians forgo a chance to ambush Wayne and his party from behind, only to be slaughtered in a face-off across a riverbank. For D. the scene was gross and malicious, calculated to make the Comanche look like tactical morons. The film had become contemptible to him, and he let me know. He'd missed the contextualizing moments that make the scene ambiguous—the other characters' dismay at Wayne's murderous fury, the bullets Wayne fires at departing braves as they carry off their dead. Nor would he happen to be in the room for the scene half an hour later when Wayne is elaborately censured for shooting an opponent in the back.

I began a defense and immediately contradicted myself, first insisting that the Indians weren't important as real presences, only as emblems of Wayne's psychic torment. The film, I tried to suggest, was a psychological epic, a diagnosis of racism through character and archetype. The Indians served as Wayne's unheeded mirror. Then, unable to leave my research on the shelf, I cited Ford's renowned accuracy. Maybe he knew a few things about Comanche battle ethics—

D. scoffed. For him it was impossible to honor Indians by showing them mowed down in a senseless slaughter (never mind that senseless slaughter was historical fact). He paced away, leaving me in a kind of hot daze, mouth dry, eyes locked on the screen, still grasping at my dream of a sanctified viewing of *The Searchers*, not seeing that it had already slipped away, that I'd again failed to defend the film, this time with an audience of just two.

D. returned, and now his trembling effort to appear casual had as much to do with the freight between us as with any junkie symptom. Rightly—he knew me well enough to sense what was coming.

"How can you expect to understand *anything* when you're too fucking distracted to give it more than a passing glance?"

"Relax, Jonathan. I only said I thought the movie wasn't very good—"

I couldn't stop. "How do you decide so easily that you're superior to a work of art? Ever worry that cheap irony won't carry you through every situation?"

"I've got eyes. It's a fifties Western."

"That's what's so pathetic about people our age—" I silenced myself before I'd widened his crimes to cover our whole generation. Still, the damage was done. D. stalked off. I wouldn't speak with him for five years from that day. Under the astonished eyes of my girlfriend I'd burst the bubble of silence in the apartment. Anger stemmed for months had risen and found a conduit. In D.'s underestimation of the film's makers I saw his underestimation of his friends, we who weren't fooled by his dissembling but indulged him, maintaining guilty silence as though we were fooled. D. had been an ambitious and generous soul when I first met him, and a champion of artistic greatness. In his sniping at *The Searchers*—at the film itself and at my galactic openness to it—I saw the slow-motion embittering of that soul condensed to one sour-grapes snapshot.

What may have astonished my girlfriend more, and shames me in retrospect, is the Nietzschean chilliness of my actions. As in a priest-and-doctor-in-a-lifeboat puzzle, two things cried for saving and I could save just one. Seeing a friend spiral into desolation I reserved my protective sympathy instead for a work of art, for John Ford and John Wayne, remote, dead, and indifferent though they might be. Again my cards were on the table. Greatness above all.

But that was in retrospect. At the time my concern was for my relationship with *The Searchers*. How ill-fated, how aggrieved, it had become. What was it with this film? Would I ever get to watch it without yelling at someone?

3. Berkeley

I snuck into the Pacific Film Archive on the heels of a crowd of perhaps fifty students, then sat with them in the theater, waiting—for what I didn't know. The screening room there is a lot like Bennington's Tishman, an austere, whisper-absorbing little hall, only built into a large museum in the center of a city instead of standing free in the Vermont woods. It was two years since my argument with D., and I was two years into the first draft of my quasi-Western. A grad-student friend, appraised of my need to refurbish my mind's eye with a constant stream of imagery, had tipped me off to the existence of an undergraduate course on the Western, mentioning that the professor who taught it had once written about *The Searchers*. So I was there that afternoon to see a screening and hear a lecture, without any clue as to what was on the syllabus.

The lights dimmed. The Warner Bros. logo, a strum of acoustic guitar, the familiar credit sequence—today's movie was *The Searchers*. Sure, why not? Sitting there anonymous among the murmuring, notebook-rustling students, I stifled a laugh. I'd been watching the movie regularly on video, in private trysts. This would be the first time in the company of others since my early disasters.

Other films can live in the tunnel-vision light of video, but *The Searchers* aches for the air of a screen large enough so that Wayne can loom like those distant towers of rock, and for the air of an audience. A ragged slice of American *something*, it wants to be met by another slice— to be projected, ideally, on a canyon wall, for a crowd of millions. The Cal freshmen at the Pacific Film Archive that afternoon were just forty or fifty shapeless new minds, there half willingly, dreaming of dates or

Frisbees, yet they gave the film the air it needed. Or maybe after five or six watchings I was ready to respond to every frame of *The Searchers*, to meet it completely. Maybe there was something freeing about my place there as an official ghost, voiceless. As the lights came up I wept discreetly.

I stayed for the professor's talk. In his lecture he gestured at the film's deep ambiguities without ever reaching, apparently with nothing to prove. He might have seemed a bit perfunctory, enclosed in a bubble of weariness, but if I noticed I blamed the bubble on the students. They were slightly interested, slightly more vague and restless. The vibrant ridicule of the Bennington students had been replaced here by automatic, spaced-out respect—sure it's an important film: It's *assigned*, isn't it? In the professor I grokked a fellow obsessive. But I mistook him for an unfulfilled obsessive, instead of the vanquished one he turned out to be.

The next day I tried not to be self-conscious, waiting in the English Department corridor behind a couple of his students. When my turn came I apologized for sneaking into his class, described the book I was writing, praised his lecture, then fished—he'd written about *The Searchers* somewhere, yes?

What I caught was an old boot of pride lodged at the bottom of a stagnant lake of academic ennui, that reflexive self-censorship of real enthusiasms. I dragged the boot up to the surface, if only for a second. "My article's about the iconography of Monument Valley," he said, with unguarded brightness. "I only published an excerpt. The long version's much more—I'm still working on it, actually—"

"I'd love to see it." I scribbled my address.

"Yes, yes . . ." But he was already slipping back into those opaque depths. He'd noticed that he ought to be bewildered to have me in his office, that he didn't really need a wild-eyed autodidact tugging his obsessions into the light. By then I was familiar with how so many grad students, hunkered down inside their terrifying careers, spoke of *teaching loads*, *job postings*, anything but the original passions at the cramped secret center of their work. Now I saw it was the same for the professor. Or worse. Armies of yawning undergraduates had killed that part of him. Long or short, published or unfinished, I never saw any version of that essay.

4. Defending *The Searchers*

I surrounded *The Searchers*, ambushed it at every pass, told it to reach for the sky. In my pursuit I watched hundreds of other Westerns, studying *the tradition*, looking for glimpses. I studied Ford, learned his language, first in good films, then in rotten ones. I watched Scorsese's *Taxi Driver*, Paul Schrader's *Hardcore*, those unofficial remakes, wanting to triangulate my obsession or feel the pulse of someone else's. I read biographies of Wayne: What made him ready to play the part? Did he understand or was he Ford's tool? I mowed through scholarship, hoping to assemble a framework that would free me to understand all I felt. And I wrote my novel; like a child with dollhouse figures I manipulated my versions of the characters and crises that had overpowered me, trying to decant *The Searchers*, unmake it, consume it. I watched the film and thought about it and talked about it too much, and when I eventually became a bore, *The Searchers* shot me in the back and walked away.

I diminished the film, I think. By overestimating it, then claiming myself as its defender, I'd invented another, more pretentious way of underestimating it. My wish to control its reception was a wish to control my own guilt and regret, not anything the film needed from me, or from anyone. If the case for *The Searchers* could be made airtight then my dropping out of Bennington was justified. My cruelty to D. excused. My own isolating intensity pined for some tidy story of struggle and triumph. But there might not actually be anything to struggle with, no triumph to claim, nobody to rescue. Wasn't it possible that John Wayne should have left Natalie Wood in the tepee—that she was happier there? Weren't he and I a couple of asses?

For years I'd chastised the crowd at Tishman in my fantasies, my words ever-more blistering, my argument ever-more seamless. Now I concocted a balm for the burning ears of my imaginary schoolmates: *I can forgive your resistance to this film.* The Searchers *is a thing I seem doomed to spend a lifetime trying to fathom, and how often do you have a lifetime to spend?* Then I'd add, *Can you forgive me my absurd responsiveness?*

Oh, I've perfected my defense of the film. It's hinged on the notion that in certain Hollywood films a major star can be placed under examination as icon of a set of neurotic symptoms, a "problematic site," and yet still operate as a creature of free will and moral relevance, a character whose choices matter. James Stewart in *Vertigo*, say, or Humphrey Bogart in *In a Lonely Place*. Refuse the notion and *The Searchers* becomes unwatchable, an explosion in the void. Grant it and the rest falls into place. The weird stuff, the racist stuff, the hysterical stuff: it all serves to split Wayne from fellow characters and from the viewer's sympathies, to foreground his lonely rage. It's very, ah, *Brechtian*. If you liked, I could chart how even the most distractingly unfunny pratfall contributes to my thesis. Imagine a DVD with my commentary, my filibuster of articulations, covering every frame.

Snore. Who'd listen? Detractors of *The Searchers* are casual snipers, not dedicated enemies—like D., or the audience at Tishman, they take a potshot and wander off, interest evaporated. Those who care like I do cherish their own interpretations, and don't need mine. I know this because as a minor consolation I've collected these people. The rock critic who screens a 16 mm print of *The Searchers* in his living room. The biographer who scoured Monument Valley to find the charred remains of the burned cabin, chunks of which he hoards at his home in L.A. Others . . . among fellow cultists the title's enough, passed like a talisman.

A new friend remarks he's surprised to learn I rate *The Searchers* as an influence.

"Have you seen it?" I ask, falsely casual.

"Long time ago. I just remember how racist it was."

"*The Searchers* is racist the way *Huckleberry Finn* is racist," I say, of course. But it's cant, and stale in my mouth. He'll watch again and understand, or not. *The Searchers* is my private club, and if you don't join you'll never know you've been rejected. I'm like the Cal professor—caring has worn me out. *The Searchers* is too gristly to be digested in my novel, too willful to be bounded in my theories. I watch or don't, doesn't matter:

The Searchers strides on, maddened, through broken landscapes incapable of containing it—Ford's oeuvre, and Wayne's, the "Studio-Era Film," and my own defeated imagination—everywhere shrugging off categories, refusing the petitions of embarrassment and taste, defying explanation or defense as only great art or great abomination ever could.

The Disappointment Artist

Mrs. Neverbody vs. Edward Dahlberg

My aunt Billie—Wilma Yeo (1918–1994) to her readers, to the world, to you—was among the first human beings I remember. Her Kansas City apartment is the site of one of my earliest, murkiest memories: seated on a carpet, I wept at seeing, on television, a depiction of a forest fire, one that routed a herd of panicked baby animals. Aunt Billie's twin daughters, then young teenagers, laughed at me for weeping. In the memory, which plays like a length of corroded celluloid—grainy, broken at both ends, but reliably identical each time—Aunt Billie sweeps in, rescues and consoles me, lightly chastises her daughters.

I lived with my parents in Kansas City, on the campus of the Kansas City Art Institute, from 1965, when I was two, until 1968, when my parents returned to New York City, and each of three or four of my earliest memories takes place there. Another involves television: taking shelter during a tornado warning, with my parents and a couple of their friends, in the basement of our stone house. George Burk, another painter on the faculty then at KCAI and my father's best friend, brought for entertainment a six-pack of beer and a portable black-and-white, on which we watched *The Monkees* while the storm harmlessly passed. Yet another Kansas City memory is of seeing my first film in a theater: *Yellow Submarine.* Counterfeit Beatles, animated Beatles, forest fires seen but unreal, tornados real but unseen—may one plead, Your Honor, post-modernism as an involuntary condition?

That's Kansas City's whole place in my life: a small, strange place. Aunt Billie's place in my life is larger. She was my first writer. And, though my father was a painter and I was trained for a career in his footsteps, as a visual artist, I somehow knew from the first to sit at the feet of any writer I encountered. Aunt Billie was primarily an author of children's books, but her résumé boasted articles in *The Reader's Digest* and *The Saturday Evening Post*, and a biography of Thomas Hart Benton, *Maverick with a Paintbrush*, which, though written simply enough for young readers, is solidly researched and a contribution to Benton studies. Her *Mrs. Neverbody's Recipes* (J. B. Lippincott, 1968; the title page notes: "The following poems were first published in *Humpty Dumpty's Magazine*") was the first autographed book in my collection, which before I was even out of my teenage years had grown to include inscriptions from Allen Ginsberg, Robert Heinlein, Norton Juster, and Anthony Burgess. I was a nerdish and sycophantic kid, let me be the first to say. I revered writers, and still do. I loved my aunt Billie.

So did my father, who's still around. Sibling bonds were strong among my father and his two sisters and three brothers. They grew up together in Depression-era towns in Missouri and Iowa. But Aunt Billie (the second oldest) and my father (the runt) enjoyed a particular lifelong kinship as the two "creative" types. Their closeness defied and outlasted my father's repeatedly throwing over the Midwest for, in turn, Columbia University, the army, Paris (on a painter's Fulbright), and New York again.

On the telephone my father still shouts, gives only rudimentary news, and suspects all he hears, feeling, perhaps rightly, that long-distance calls are a sham apparatus. He and Aunt Billie maintained their intimacy by writing letters. One day not long ago my father asked if I'd ever heard of Edward Dahlberg. I had some familiarity with that name, but I couldn't imagine why he wanted to know.

"Have a look at this," he said, and handed me the letter.

Dearest Brother—first of all I should say that I write this in an ego-centered search for an identity that I lost in a class at UMKC taught by Edward Dahlberg, a writer in residence for this semester. To describe him is impossible—I've read most of his autobiography now BECAUSE I WAS FLESH, and have a little more comprehension of this individual who emerged from a poverty stricken childhood in Kansas City where his whore-mother was a Star Lady Barber and he had no father—his book is the story of Lizzie Dahlberg—his mother—whom he loved with revulsion. This man, an intellectual Alexander King—in both looks and attitude—bitter, bitter sweet (and I don't use the term intellectual in the bannal method of today) has verbally crucified every member of the class who dared open his mouth—and to read a work of ones own! Sheer folly. He is a man of letters and so well acquainted with Dreiser, Swift, Mather, Taylor, Stendhal, DeBalzac, Unamuno, Dryden, Gissing, Ruskin, Morris, Ford, Coleridge, Anderson, Baudouin, Flaubert, Keats, Gill, Read, Chestov, Thoreau, Rozanov, Merjkowski, Tolstoi Swinburne, Hulme, Williams, Heywood, Jastrow, (all of the bible) though he disclaims religion Weaver, Meyers, Garland, Berkman, Goldman, Delacroix, Dostovsky etc but not many more—that he is astonishingly like a walking library—He calls James and Brecht scribblers—says nothing worth reading has been written 'en contemporary . . . no doubt it would seem to be a mistake to sit two hours twice a week in the mezermizing world he weaves for I can no longer write a word—should my life depend on it.

That's the whole text of the first, unparagraphed page. There are six more. The letter—it is still in my possession—is on onionskin, letters carved in ink by a manual's keys. Rich with delirious typos and misspellings (Dostovsky and Chestov!), and hasty cursive annotations, as well as a torrent of weirdly antique name-drops (Alexander King, Jastrow), but above all eloquently desperate, the letter radiates human intellectual panic like pheromones. Each time I read it I feel the thrill of unsealing a time capsule, and of awakening my aunt from her deservedly peaceful slumber.

The year of the letter is 1965, identifiable by Aunt Billie's stated age and some family chatter on the last few pages. Wilma Yeo was forty-eight, still three years from placing *Mrs. Neverbody's Recipes*, her first book, with Lippincott, when she had her bracing encounter with Dahlberg.

_____

Edward Dahlberg (1900–1977) was born, illegitimately, in Boston and raised in Kansas City (Dahlberg: "Let me admit it, I hate Kansas City"). His tormented coming-of-age, split between a Jewish orphanage and the home of his mother, the barber and adventuress described by Wilma Yeo, is the center of both his first novel, *Bottom Dogs* (1934), famously introduced by D. H. Lawrence (Dahlberg: "I wasn't influenced by Lawrence at all! That's a small, wanton, niggardly conjecture!"), and his late memoir, *Because I Was Flesh* (1964). Where Dahlberg is remembered, *Because I Was Flesh* is accounted his masterpiece. His career was split. There were three novels in the thirties, full of ancient slang and proto–Hubert Selby grubbiness, good enough to make him a signal figure in the largely forgotten—and, by Dahlberg, regretted—proletarian movement; then, some years of wandering, followed by reinvention as a crypto-classical mandarin stylist, no longer committed to fiction but to literary-historical essays, memoirs, mythological poetry, and fulmination. In this late phase, Dahlberg enjoyed (a uniquely inappropriate word) a reputation as an underground hero of American writing—an unwilling father to Beats ("I have no feeling about these boys. But they are doing what was done thirty years ago and they imagine they are avant-garde. You can be scatological in any century; it is not news. Or a dung-eater anytime; it is an old habit"), and a figure legendary for his auto-exile, his excoriating intolerance of other writers. Dahlberg routinely broadcast, on every channel open to him, a galactic disappointment with his own career and with the bad flavor living had left in his mouth. He died in 1977, his last jottings satires of the television commercials which had come to fascinate him.

I'd known the name, faintly. Working in used bookshops, I'd fondled a few Dahlberg tomes before slashing their prices or consigning them to bins of the never-to-be-sold. I associated him with the agony of the rebuffed career, the refused book. In used bookselling one becomes a dowser of the underground river of refused books, and the dowsing rod twitches like the second hand of a clock. Expertise is knowing which few, of the thousands flung to posterity by their flap copy, anyone would ever actually pay to read. So, Dahlberg: a guilty association, another titan I'd dissed by thinking him a drag on the retail flow.

Aunt Billie's letter concentrated my attention. Dahlberg's, it seemed, was a shrill, vibrant voice clinging to the edge of the collective literary consciousness—just. As I asked around, seeking to see how his name played among my best-read friends, the answer was always the one I'd have given myself: Dahlberg, oh yeah, always meant to find out what he was about. I located a biography, *The Wages of Expectation*, by Charles DeFanti, and *Edward Dahlberg: A Tribute*, a Festschrift assembled by Jonathan Williams; the most recent item was "Broaching Difficult Dahlberg," by Lydia Davis, an essay, published in *Conjunctions*, which circles Dahlberg without actually plunging in. There, Davis interrogates older writers still bearing grudges against Dahlberg, confirming the testimony of the biography and of many of Dahlberg's own ostensible supporters: this was a more than moderately difficult man. And Dahlberg's tendency to be recalled but unread made him a bizarre discovery, a writer whose reputation was either blinking out of existence at the exact moment I'd located it, or, weirder, a writer whose reputation was somehow *frozen in the act of blinking out of existence.*

The more I looked, the more it seemed Dahlberg's compulsion for taking out his monstrous disappointment on any human within striking distance was the only reputation left, dragging the books distantly behind it. Dahlberg's biographer, Charles DeFanti, in *The Wages of Expectation* details how Dahlberg denounced as unworthy, at various times, Charles Olson, Allen Ginsberg, Theodore Dreiser ("If I had reread his books, I would have had to assail him"), Robert Graves, Edmund Wilson, and dozens of others, all attempted friends or sponsors of Dahlberg's career. Here's Paul Carroll, in his Introduction to *The Edward Dahlberg Reader*, witnessing a Dahlberg performance at a cocktail party given in his honor: "What he said about Hemingway, Faulkner, Eliot, Wilson, Pound . . . was univocal, brilliant, sour, erudite, and unanswerable. Only the cadence of his sentences . . . seemed to keep Dahlberg's words from becoming a scream." The list can seem endless, but to eliminate any uncertainty,

SIMMS LIBRARY ALBUQUERQUE ACADEMY

Dahlberg sweepingly denounced not only the whole twentieth century's shelf, but the nineteenth century's as well, locating the corruption of American literature well before Melville. As for his personal relations, he made himself famous for his cold shoulder, arranging elaborate fallings-out so persistently that William O'Rourke, a student and disciple, eulogized him this way: "Edward Dahlberg wrote 18 books and one masterpiece that will endure; at the end of his long life he had less than six people he would have called friend." Perhaps my aunt Billie had had the privilege of having her head bitten off not by some average writing-class ogre but by the greatest head biter of all time, the Ozzy Osbourne of writing-teaching.

> When you listen to him talk—where do I, a woman of forty eight, with so little time (comparatively speaking) (and he answers— "there is not such thing as time"—Life is an error and death the only truth etc.)—Fit in this picture? His theory that only children are knowing—and that we innundate our minds with every passing minute and thus die with each experience—never able to change our life's destiny one drop—never again able to attain what we lost through living—is near a parallel that I have long ago reached—and the reason that I want to write for children and believe that it is the hardest writing to do.

She then adds,

> But when I try to discuss writing for children, he says there is no such thing—write what you have to say and pray to God that children will read it . . . Now this is fine—I go along—but how can I go when I have suddenly lost my way to anyplace at all? I write *you* this because, knowing how many classes you have sat through— where, undoubtedly this same kind of person, taught—I wonder if you can help me. I guess what I want you to say is Don't Listen To Him, but it's too late for that because I already have. How far should one go in deciding what one's personal limitations are, and settling for less than perfection. If I read all of these things (I

don't literally mean every book, but read, say for a year or two) and quit writing (as I seem to have anyway) do you think I would be happier (ugh what a weak word—of course the only happiness is satisfaction or joy in work in progress—and the ability to move on to the next job without looking back with too many weakening day-dreams.) But just when I thought I was going along so great—I've stubbed my mental toe! On a rock! You know that for several years I've been reading deeper things—I can finally read poetry—a little—after years of trying to . . . I can recognize good passages—I've learned the effectiveness of small words—found the art in brevity—doubted the adjective—learned to discriminate in the varying shades of words . . . increased my sad little vocabulary some . . . but can one really know what is good unless one has long looked upon perfection until anything less seems shoddy and factory made.

To attempt to read Dahlberg, as I began to do, is to find oneself reading about him instead. For a writer whose persistent epiphany was isolation ("All intelligent Americans are extremely alone"), and whose obsession it was to decry the charlatanism of comradeship among writers ("I am not looking for disciples. Jesus did not even know what to do with the apostles, and they had such dull auditory nerves that they could not hear what came from his soul"), Dahlberg is nevertheless one of the *most introduced* writers of all time. The parade of ushers begins, of course, with *Bottom Dogs*. It turns out that D. H. Lawrence's essay was commissioned; Davis judges it "unwilling," DeFanti "squeamish if not somewhat petulant." Reasonable enough: Lawrence's envoi to Dahlberg's career concludes, "I don't want to read any more books like this."

Lawrence there inaugurates a great tradition: Dahlberg is routinely assassinated by his own apologists. Here's Gerald Burns, in an Afterword to *The Leafless American and Other Writings* (a book consisting of a hundred pages of Dahlberg, a Preface by Robert Creeley, and an Introduction by Harold Billings, on top of the Afterword!): "I have heard he was down on blacks, and the reason seems to be that they have made bastions of our apartments and robbed us of the parks . . . [he] says the faces of their children show why they do not yet have a civilization." Karl Shapiro, from *Edward Dahlberg: A Tribute*: "His petulance and misunderstanding of the Modern are one thing; his disgust for . . . modern art and literature must be brushed aside; but his blind loyalty to himself as a poet, prophet, and *l'inconnu*—these are his birthright, by all means." Jonathan Williams, in the same book, gratuitously disinters what may seem a too telling review by Alden Whitman in *The New York Times*: "Dahlberg is outrageous, a deliberate striver for shock value, a magpie who delights to show off his gleanings from the classics, a bombast on occasion, a writer of ponderous nonsense and almost insufferable ego." Well, ahem.

These same supporters compensate by overstatement. In this, they have encouragement from Dahlberg's style itself. His absolutism is recapitulated every place he's remembered. Paul Carroll: "Is there any author living who is even in the same country as Edward Dahlberg in the moral grandeur and violence of his writings?" Ronald Johnson: "I sometimes wonder whether we deserve an Edward Dahlberg to reprimand and cajole us." August Derleth: "He is as much a genius as anyone of whom I can think, past or present . . ." To invest in Dahlberg is to adopt scorched-earthism.

In a letter dated September 2, 1964, anticipating his departure from Ireland for Kansas City, to teach my aunt's class, Dahlberg wrote:

"Good teaching is apocalyptic talking."

Again, Wilma Yeo:

There is a young man in the class who looks so much like you, Dick, that when I watch his eyes as he reads (as he made the grave mistake of doing) one of his poems—I am where you are! Drivel! Says the old prof! Pure drivel! You don't even know that you don't know anything—read, read, read!!!! I, of course, had thought it quite good. He will say, "Did you bring a paper? On what book—"

"It's a creative paper."

"How do you know it is creative? Oh well, read it."

Then he interrupts about the second word and says, "Forgive me, I don't want to be rude but that is asinine and puerile and we don't have time to waste on it." or "that word makes me want to vomit." I know you say, why listen? but he has something to say. His book is good—his soul is bitter. A boiled prune without hope or belief. Since I can't write, I have been drawing. This is something I understand why I can't do well, and so I can enjoy it.

My aunt then describes some other published writers at Dahlberg's mercy, including Alice Winter, author of *The Velvet Bubble*, and Frankie Wu, a poet who had already placed work with *The New Yorker*:

He doesn't know any of the three of us have ever sold anything and wouldn't care if he did, for he believes that writing to sell is as morbid as you feel that commercial art is—and that could easily be true, but writing is of so little use in a file cabinet . . . anyway, Frankie typed off this same poem and handed it in—a non-poem, he said, with three good lines in it—but he is interested in Frankie—partly because he likes Orientals and thinks America would be better off if we had let them in—and maybe a little because of that poem, but he was so intense in his criticism of it, in front of the class that she was ill afterward—Frankie has a rare disease and spent four years in an iron lung—her husband Dr. Wu is a quite famous brain surgeon or she would probably not be alive. It is a disease of the nerve endings and sometimes affects her as if she had been drinking. If he is too cruel to her, Alice or I shall probably tell him to go to hell. Kindly—for he is easily hurt, as people so often are who persist in <u>brutal</u> frankness.

There! It was out and said, though only scrawled between margins at the last moment, as though Wilma Yeo could no more bring herself to omit her diagnosis than she could bear to judge her teacher: *a boiled prune, easily hurt.* Or, in the words of Josephine Herbst: "There is so much that is paradoxical, quixotic, contrary about Edward Dahlberg . . . is it possible always to agree with him? Or to share his exclusive literary tastes? But there is consistency in his inconsistency . . . what writer is less afraid of absurdities or willing to show himself as ridiculous?" What compelled my aunt Billie, then, beyond her necessary rejection of what he told her—evidently, "quit writing"—was Dahlberg's vulnerability. Wasn't that right, and couldn't it be enough? Wasn't Edward Dahlberg not-so-secretly tender, and didn't his genius spring from that pained source, in a very *Wound and the Bow* sort of way? Perhaps I could forgive him, and begin to read him.

Perhaps I was about to do so. But then I found the next two pieces of evidence in my search. First, a letter from Piers Paul Read, who studied with Dahlberg at Columbia in 1967 and whose father, Sir Herbert Read, was one of Dahlberg's staunch supporters:

> My misgivings about Dahlberg as a teacher were amply fulfilled. He had a bullying manner and a total intolerance of any writing but his own. He had read my first novel . . . which had already been published by this time and rejected it as worthless in front of the class . . . We more or less made up the quarrel . . . he was not, however, a man to be ignored and he continued to bully me—saying, at one time, in front of the class, that I was responsible for my father's cancer because I had been married in Strasbourg!

My second discovery was a memoir by William O'Rourke, who, incredibly, had been part of the Kansas City class my aunt attended. O'Rourke paints the scene in Dahlbergian tones: "Women filled his classes. Cameoed dowagers with roughed jowls and red velvet capes, young brittle-lipped girls whose pens took notes nodding like steadfast crochet needles." Women, it needs to be noted, are the ultimate Dahlbergian sore point. Dahlberg's greatest subject was his mother, and his great lifelong Waterloo was his own sexual appetite—his seven marriages, various imputations of harassment and physical abuse, and his whole raging ambivalence about sex:

> A man may want to study Mark or Paracelsus, or go on an errand to do a kindness to an aging woman, but this tyrant [the penis] wants to discharge itself either because the etesian gales are acerb

or a wench has just stooped over to gather her laundry . . . the head is so obtuse as to go absolutely crazy over a pair of hunkers, which is no more than a chine of beef.

And, as elsewhere, his admirers eagerly hoist him to the heavens on this petard. Thus, O'Rourke continues:

> The writing class had decomposed to a half dozen. Another male, a speech teacher . . . and an assortment of female poets. Dahlberg sat with his legs crossed with gray exhaustion over his face . . . when a woman volunteered to read a children's book she had written. He had spoken against the children's dilution of the Classics before, but consented with alarm for there were no other offerings during the period. She began:
>
> "Winnie was a puppy who looked like a mop and rode the elevators of downtown Kansas City until everybody knew his name . . ."
>
> Edward Dahlberg, American Artist, sat with his head shrouded by his hands.
>
> She continued:
>
> "He would walk around the Plaza, for he lived with his master in an apartment . . ."
>
> "Stop," he said, hardly audible. "Stop. Please."

Stop, please! indeed. What was this compulsion? What did the letter mean to *me*? In my exaggerated relish and mock horror at uncovering Dahlberg's heroic monstrosity I was becoming a student of Dahlberg myself, another slave pining for his lash. Worse, in my compulsion to vengeance on my aunt's behalf, I resembled not a follower but old grudge-nurturing, injury-cherishing Dahlberg himself.

That the writing workshop, the sort led by an established writer and populated by aspirants, is a site of human longing and despair is undeniable. Fear and loathing, the grosser undercurrents of hostility, fratricidal and patri- or matri-cidal impulses, fox-in-the-henhouse-ish preying on one's own potential successors, those are more like secret poxes—venereal flare-ups, to use a comparison beloved by Dahlberg. The famous teacher who steals from his students—that's a story going around. Alternately, one hears of the writer with the former protégé, one extensively favored with opportunities, opened doors, who's now, after publication, brushed his mentor off—but only after making an unacknowledged appropriation of signature aspects of the elder writer's live-performance shtick. Typically, in our correct, passive-aggressive era, hostility has gone underground. The last remaining interrupters, ranters, tantrum artists—and a handful do still roam the creative-writing landscape—are mentioned with the tittering that disguises our uneasy awe. No one approximately my own age will tell even his or her worst student, as Dahlberg often apparently told his very best, that they are simply not a writer, that they ought to give it up. And every one of us feels a queasy guilt at this hesitation: Are we perhaps only leaving that job to be done by some subsequent disenchanter—an editor, or a series of rejection slips, a teacher braver than ourselves? Are we like bogus farmers, raising crops already scheduled to be destroyed in some government buyout?

So we smile in the classroom and work out murkier feelings among ourselves. Tongues scarred with bite marks, then loosened by a little red wine, wag in late-night gripe sessions. A few teachers circulate excerpts from the laughably inept, others memorize the unforgettable lines. A prizewinning poet shocked me years ago, explaining casually, almost sweetly, that the majority of her students could be shown how to write an adequate, competent poem—the problem was few of these poems would ever be anything but too "boring" to read. The ferocity and finality of that modifier wasn't lost on me. A cheery type (at least by Dahlbergian standards), I like many of my students personally. Their striving mostly stirs me, often inspires me, sporadically breaks my heart. Yet I participate in the venting too, and in the whispered framing of guilty questions: Is it for anything but the paycheck that we go on propagating this farce?

We're all of us, students and teachers, stranded in the breach between the violently solitary and elitist necessities of High Art—exemplified, in our time, by professional Bartlebys of the William Gass or Cynthia Ozick type—and the Horatio Alger wishfulness of so much writing advice, the self-actualizing egalitarianism of *Writer's Digest*. Yet faced with this ubiquitous hunger even to be allowed the attempt to make oneself a writer—so human and poignant, so profoundly benign—what does it mean to install a Dahlberg in a classroom and permit him to maul a Yeo? What's the value of the dissident writer, one who exiles himself from contemporaries, audience, and apprentices, in the cultural marketplace? Why do we—*why did my aunt*—seem to cherish our brushes with Dahlbergs, even as we encourage their victims to complain them out of the profession?

Edward Dahlberg—for I've finally begun to read him—was a genius, sure. Having penetrated the haze of remorse around his career, I've joined the tinny chorus: *Because I Was Flesh*, his memoir of Kansas City childhood and orphanhood, but most of all a portrait of his disreputable, unbearable, and resolutely life-embracing mother, is a great book. Great in the saddest and simplest way, for Dahlberg has arrayed an armor of rhetoric to fend off his pain, and everywhere the armor proves inadequate. *Because I Was Flesh* is a catalogue of defenseless defenses, of feeble snarling assaults on implacable, if erratic, love. It shows Dahlberg's baroque scalpel turned inward, for once. Dahlberg would certainly have loathed our contemporary culture of brandished trauma. Yet brandished trauma is his legacy:

She did not know what to do with her life or with her feelings. She toiled because she was afraid to starve, and because she had nothing else to do; but her will was too sick to love the child of her lust. He was so skinny and yellow that his nose seemed to cover his face; and all the obduracy that was in her short, round neck had passed over to him. If he saw a speck on the wall, he imagined that it was the ordure of flies. When he looked at the greasy, rotten oilcloth on the table, he would not touch his scummy soup. His mind gave him intolerable pain when he thought of the back alley that lay between 8th and 7th where he had seen gross rodents. On occasion, when he heard the chirruping of rats in the basement of the building or in the rear of the shop, his face grew more peaked and rancid, and he buried his head in his arms and retched. Lizzie was unable to comprehend his nausea, for like most people of her class in the Midwest she found a certain amount of rapture in looking at vermin. Often the lady barbers spoke at great length about loathsome creatures, and the boy listened and could not leave off hearing what made him green and sick for weeks.

All that Lizzie could understand was that the child of her profligacy vomited and that he would grow up ugly . . .

Because I Was Flesh is all the more moving for how late it comes, for the sense that Dahlberg had had to taunt himself into writing a masterpiece by declaring himself a neglected master for thirty years before he'd written one. And how fascinating, how instructive, that his first pass at the material of his great book is rehearsed in such different form in his first, *Bottom Dogs*. All the "proletarian" moves of *Bottom Dogs*—the wallowing sociology, the overemphatic slang, now so quaint—serve to show how useless the consolation of any sort of crowd, or movement, or fraternity with his fellow man would ever be to Dahlberg in the long run. Though *Because I Was Flesh* may seem to be written in a more "pretentious" style, compared to the ostensible street authenticity of *Bottom Dogs*, it is the latter book which wrecks the earlier's pretensions. Screw the proles, *Flesh* says: I want my mama—except my mama, and my yearning for her, are beneath my respect.

In his other work Dahlberg was only a bizarre, sometimes hypnotic stylist, and a writer who forgot to love anything better than his own failure. His literary and cultural criticism, in *Can These Bones Live?*, *The Leafless American*, and elsewhere, is worse than useless, it's corrupt—poisoned by his reeling distress. His parable of disenchantment with the left, *The Flea of Sodom*, is unreadably arcane—for a lucid portrait of the intelligentsia's sad contortions in the 1930s, better turn to Lionel Trilling's *The Middle of the Journey* or Paula Fox's *The Western Coast*. Beyond the autobiographical books, only *The Sorrows of Priapus*, a kooky diatribe against the human body and sexual desire, is worth a look, and that because it reveals a gift for comedy, a voice so overwrought with self-alienation it anticipates the morbid hilarity of Donald Antrim or Ben Marcus:

The phallus is a slovenly bag created without intellect or ontolog-
ical purpose or design, and as long as the human being has this
hanging worm appended to his middle, which is no good for anything except passing urine and getting a few, miserable irritations,
for which he forsakes his mother, his father, and his friends, he
will never comprehend the Cosmos.

The problem is that, apart from his childhood, Dahlberg has just two
subjects: his own career's undervaluation and the emptiness of existence.
Since he was American, contemporary, and literary, it is largely contemporary American literary existence that is decried, but one quickly sniffs
out how ready he is to spread the bad news to cover anything alerted to
his gaze: home, travel, youth, age, company, loneliness, and girls, girls,
girls. D. H. Lawrence, in a letter written out of exhaustion with the
younger writer's preening complaints: "for HEAVEN'S SAKE LEAVE
OFF BEING UNLUCKY—you seem to ask for it." Dahlberg reportedly
quoted the line with pride. He recognized early on that despair was his
gift, and he gave it freely—in fact he'd sling it at your departing back.

So despite the lasting beauty of the one towering book, the fame of
Dahlberg's terror campaign through literary culture is no mistake. His
failure was greater than his greatness: Dahlberg was a disappointment
artist. His virulence against professional glad-handing was only a matter
of dynamiting fish in a barrel, as any easy joke about logrolling blurbists
has by now more than demonstrated. Dahlberg's deeper dissidence was
against reassurance and consolation, even in their purest forms. That
when he considered Hart Crane and William Carlos Williams and
Theodore Dreiser he saw only their failure was a confession of pain; the
deepest he could afford to offer as to how little writing a masterpiece
could assuage the howling loneliness of that needless stint in the Kansas
City orphanage. If only a handful of readers, or garlands, was too few, a
million readers, or ten million, could never have been enough.

Dahlberg's special achievement was to take this rage and leave it raw,
refuse to professionalize it. Gilbert Sorrentino wrote:

Dahlberg's bitterness and sourness are familiar to many readers, as is his scornful treatment of writers who offend his sensibilities. His near to comic reactionary positions on anything and everything are equally well known. But what does it matter after all? . . . You can find no meaning in Dahlberg, none that you can't get from a thousand lesser writers. Mailer is a titanic thinker next to him; your mailman or boss has more enlightened or informed ideas. There is nothing in Dahlberg except his greatness; he is the real thing . . . The only thing you can do with Dahlberg is read him.

Again, as everywhere, the objections come first: the "comic reactionary positions."

Dahlberg wed the kill-the-father imperative, the famous anxiety of influence, to the truism that a man is only as big as his enemies. Therefore: if one wished to be the greatest writer of the twentieth century, simply make an enemy of the whole of contemporary literature. Dahlberg spent the first two-thirds of his life measuring his fellows by Melville and finding them not only wanting but bankrupt. Then, in his late fifties, in an act of almost majestic inconsistency, he turned on Melville, declaring his "failure" as well. By doing so, Dahlberg comically exposed the faulty premises in that whole rigged game: to exalt himself he'd forged the obligation to *hate greatness*. Relishing literature's variety of methods and discourse—watching a thousand flowers bloom—simply wasn't an option. Dahlberg left himself no margin to consider that Faulkner, Beckett, Joyce, and so many rejected others might be his life's companions, his colleagues, his company. Not to mention his masters.

Novelists pin their disgust to straw men every day, in this or that review. Others weep for the Death of the Novel. The Herculean instinct to clear the stables prospers in us all from time to time. Loathing other writers, whether they be one's teachers or students or colleagues, is likely as basic as Freud's "narcissism of minor difference," which explains that we are obliged to denounce those most similar to us because the resemblances are too telling of our vulnerabilities, our wants. Only Dahlberg did us the favor of tipping *his* narcissism of minor difference into the realm of absurdist tantrum-art, sustained for a lifetime. And what he did in burning down the veil of diffident fraternity, he did for the writing classroom as well. Other Famous Monsters of Creative-Writing Land have been known to craft their intolerance into seductive S&M ritual, binding apprentices to grueling discipleships invariably destined for wrenching betrayal. Not Dahlberg. He was as revolted by the students who were turned on by his abuse as he was by those who resisted. Every head had to come off, every supplicant cast into the wilderness. If all of us writing teachers are emperors with no clothes, it was Dahlberg who railed in starkest agony of that fact, rending his invisible garments to tatters until his constituency was forced to bellow at him that he was naked.

In 1965, the year of the letter, Wilma Yeo founded the Kansas City Writers' Group, who dedicated their 1994 anthology, *Beginning from the Middle*, to Yeo, just before her death. The Foreword explains:

> Every piece of this book is a commitment from people who love words and love to write. Wilma Yeo began a class for people who needed encouragement with writing . . . Lawyers, nurses, teachers, psychologists, editors, artists, chemical engineers—these are some of the professions in our group. But when we meet together, our real life is simply writing.

The dedication quotes Yeo's credo: "In offering a critique, you must be honest and kind. To be dishonest is to be unkind. And, to be unkind is to be dishonest to yourself and your art." Here is the sort of nurturance Edward Dahlberg resolutely denounced as false. Yet by his absolute rejection of her offer of discipleship, so excruciatingly detailed in the letter, Dahlberg authorized a forty-eight-year-old woman—instantly, it would appear—to declare herself the kind of writer, and writing teacher, she needed to be. My aunt had already "doubted the adjective" and "learned to discriminate in the varying shades of words," and she didn't need what Unamuno or Ruskin, not to mention "Chestov" or "Dostovsky" or Dahlberg had to tell her, in order to go forward. The woman could spot a boiled prune when she met one. Here's the last poem from *Mrs. Neverbody's Recipes*:

Mrs. Neverbody's Recipe for Making Crocodile Tears

To a slice of hanky-panky
Add some artificial cranky.
Moisten well with canned boo-hoo.
Flavor with a spoof or two.
Drip this slowly—as it falls
Roll it into little bawls.
If you're careful, while they're cooling
You can spread on only-fooling.
*(This recipe is not worthwhile
Unless you are a crocodile.)*

Do you feel the generosity, perhaps even forgiveness, in that last parenthetical couplet? I do. Let it be said: attending creative writing classes ennobles the brave dreamy souls who populate them, publication is a sweet and harmless church, and a minuscule handful of (presently unknown) persons will write something worth reading even during their lifetimes, let alone after. Edward Dahlberg, Worthwhile Crocodile, contributed one book readers may wish to retrieve from the bog of his disappointment, rage, sheer unpleasantness—or they may not wish to bother. His failure, though, is immortal.

13, 1977, 21

1. In the summer of 1977 I saw *Star Wars*—the original, which is all I want to discuss here—twenty-one times. Better to blurt this at the start so I'm less tempted to retreat from what still seems to me a sort of raw, howling confession, one I've long hidden in shame. Again, to pin myself like a Nabokovian butterfly (no high-lit reference is going to bail me out here, I know) to my page in geek history: I watched *Star Wars* twenty-one times in the space of four months. I was that kid alone in the ticket line, slipping past ushers who'd begun to recognize me, muttering in impatience at a urinal before finding my favorite seat. That was me, occult as a porn customer, yes, though I've sometimes denied it. Now, a quarter-century later, I'm ready for my close-up. Sort of.

2. That year I was thirteen, and likely as ideal an audience member as any mogul could have drooled for. Say every kid in the United States with even the passingest fondness for comic books or adventure fiction, *any kid with a television, even*, had bought a ticket for the same film in a single summer: blah, blah, right, that's what happened. So figure that for every hundred kids who traveled an ordinary path (*Cool movie, wouldn't mind seeing it again with my friends*) there might be one who'd make

himself ill returning to the cookie jar five or six times (*It's really still good the fourth time, I swear!*) before copping to a tummy ache. Next figure that for each *five* hundred, one or two would slip into some brain-warped identificatory obsession (*I am* Star Wars, Star Wars *am me, goo goo ga joob*) and return to the primal site often enough to push into the realm of trance and memorization. That's me, with my gaudy *twenty-one*, like DiMaggio's *fifty-six*. But what actually occurred within the secret brackets of that experience? What emotions lurk within that ludicrous temple of hours? *What the fuck was I thinking?*

3. Every one of those twenty-one viewings took place at the Loew's Astor Plaza on Forty-fourth Street, just off Times Square. I'd never seen a movie there before (and unless you count *The Empire Strikes Back*, I didn't again until 1999—*The Matrix*). And I've still never seen *Star Wars* anywhere else. The Astor Plaza was a low, deep-stretched hall with a massive screen and state-of-the-art sound, and newly enough renovated to be free of too much soda-rotted carpet, a plague among New York theaters those days. Though architecturally undistinguished, it was a superior place to see anything, I suppose. But for me it was a shrine meant for just one purpose—I took it as weirdly significant that "Astor" could be rearranged into "astro"—and in a very *New Yorker*–coverish way I believed it to be the only real and right place to see *Star Wars*, the very ground zero of the phenomenon. I felt a definite but not at all urgent pity for any benighted fools stuck watching it elsewhere. I think I associated the Astor Plaza with the Death Star, in a way. Getting in always felt like an accomplishment, both elevating and slightly dangerous.

4. Along those lines I should say it was vaguely unnerving to be a white kid in spectacles routinely visiting Times Square by subway in the middle of the 1970s. Nobody ever said anything clearly about what was wrong or fascinating about that part of the city we lived in—the information was absorbed in hints and mutterings from a polyphony of sources. In fact, though I was conscious of a certain seamy energy in those acres of sex shows and drug dealers and their furtive sidewalk customers, I was never once hassled (and this was a time when my home neighborhood, in Brooklyn, was a minefield for me personally). But the zone's reputation ensured I'd always plan my visits to fall wholly within summer's long daylight hours.

5. Problem: it doesn't seem at all likely that I went to the movie alone the first time, but I can't remember who I was with. I've polled a few of my likeliest friends from that period, but they're unable to help. In truth I can't recall a "first time" in any real sense, though I do retain a flash memory of the moment the prologue first began to crawl in tilted perspective up the screen, an Alice-in-Wonderland doorway to dream. I'd been so primed, so attuned and ready to love it (I remember mocking my friend Evan for his thinking that the title meant it was going to be some kind of all-star cavalcade of a comedy, like *It's a Mad Mad Mad Mad World* or *Smokey and the Bandit*) that my first time was gulped impatiently, then covered quickly in the memory of return visits. From the first I was "seeing it again." I think this memory glitch is significant. I associate it with my practice of bluffing familiarity with various drug experiences, later (not much later). My refusal to recall or admit to a first time was an assertion of maturity: I was *always already* a *Star Wars* fanatic.

6. I didn't buy twenty-one tickets. My count was amassed by seeing the movie twice in a day over and over again. And one famous day (famous to myself) I sat through it three times. That practice of seeing a film twice through originated earlier. Somebody—my mother?—had floated the idea that it wasn't important to be on time for a movie, or even to check the screening times before going. Instead, moviegoing in Brooklyn Heights or on Fulton Street with my brother or with friends, we'd pop in at any point in the story, watch to the end, then sit through the break and watch the beginning. Which led naturally, if the film was any good, to staying past the original point of entry to see the end twice. Which itself led to routinely twice-watching a movie we liked, even if we hadn't been late. This was encouraged, partly according to a general *Steal This Book*–ish anticapitalist imperative for taking freebies in my parents' circle in the seventies. Of course somebody—my mother?—had also figured out a convenient way to get the kids out of the house for long stretches.

7. I hate arriving late for movies now and would never watch one in this broken fashion. (It seems to me, though, that I probably learned something about the construction of narratives from the practice.) The life-long moviegoing habit which does originate for me with *Star Wars* is that of sitting in movie theaters alone. I probably only had company in the Loew's Astor Plaza four or five times. The rest of my visits were solitary, which is certainly central to any guesses I'd make about the emotional meaning of the ritual viewings.

8. I still go to the movies alone, all the time. In the absenting of self which results—so different from the quality of solitude at my writing desk—this seems to me as near as I come in my life to any reverent or worshipful or meditational practice. That's not to say it isn't also indulgent, with a frisson of guilt, of stolen privilege, every time. I'm acutely conscious of this joyous guilt in the fact that when as a solitary movie-goer I take a break to go to the bathroom *I can return to another part of the theater and watch from a different seat.* I first discovered this thrill during my *Star Wars* summer, and it's one which never diminishes. The rupture of the spectator's contract with perspective feels as transgressive as wife-swapping.

9. The function or dysfunction of my *Star Wars* obsession was paradoxical. I was using the movie as a place to hide, sure. That's obvious. At the same time, this activity of hiding inside the Loew's Astor Plaza, and inside my private, *deeper-than-yours, deeper-than-anyone's* communion with the film itself, was something I boasted widely about. By building my lamebrain World Record for screenings (fat chance, I learned later) I was teaching myself to package my own craving for solitude, and my own obsessive tendencies, as something to be admired. *You can't join me inside this box where I hide,* I was saying, *but you sure can praise the box. You're permitted to marvel at me for going inside.*

10. What I was hiding from is easy, though. My parents had separated a couple of years earlier. Then my mother had begun having seizures, been diagnosed with a brain tumor, and had had the first of two surgeries. The

summer of *Star Wars* she was five or six months from the second, unsuccessful surgery, and a year from dying.

11. I took my brother, and he stayed through it twice. We may have done that together more than once—neither of us clearly remembers. I took a girl, on a quasi-date: Alissa, the sister of my best friend, Joel. I took my mother. I tried to take my grandmother.

12. That same summer I once followed Alissa to a ballet class at Carnegie Hall and hung around the studio, expressing a polite curiosity which was cover for another, less polite curiosity. The instructor was misled or chose to misunderstand—a thirteen-year-old boy willing to set foot inside a ballet studio was a commodity, a raw material. I was offered free classes, and the teacher called my house and strong-armed my parents. I remember vividly my mother's pleasure in refusing on my behalf—I was too much of a coward—and how strongly she fastened on the fact that my visit had had nothing to do with any interest in ballet. For years this seemed to me an inexplicable cruelty in my mother toward the ballet teacher. Later I understood that in those first years of adolescence I was giving off a lot of signals to my parents that I might be gay. I was a delicate, obedient, and bookish kid, a constant teacher's pet. Earlier that year my father had questioned me regarding a series of distended cartoon noses I'd drawn in ballpoint on my loose-leaf binder—they had come out looking a lot like penises. And my proclaimed favorite *Star Wars* character was the tweaking English robot, C-3PO.

13. I did and do find C-3PO sexy. It's as if a strand of DNA from Fritz Lang's fetishized girl robot in *Metropolis* has carried forward to the bland world of *Star Wars*. Also, whereas Carrie Fisher's robes went to her ankles, C-3PO is obviously naked, and ashamed of it.

14. Alissa thought the movie was okay (my overstated claims generally cued a compensating shrug in others) and that was our last date, if it was a date. We're friends now.

15. I don't know how much of an effort it was for my mother to travel by subway to a movie theater in Manhattan by the summer of '77, but I do know it was unusual, and that she was certainly doing it to oblige me. It might have been one of our last ventures out together, before it was impossible for her. I remember fussing over rituals inside the theater, showing her my favorite seat, and straining not to watch her watch it throughout, not to hang on her every reaction. Afterward she too found the movie just okay. It wasn't her kind of thing, but she could understand why I liked it so much. Those were pretty close to her exact words. Maybe with her characteristic Queens hard-boiled tone: *I see why you like it, kiddo.* Then, in a turn I find painful to relate, she left me there to watch it a second time, and took the subway home alone. What a heartbreaking rehearsal! I was saying, in effect: *Come and see my future, post-mom self. Enact with me your parting from it. Here's the world of cinema and stories and obsessive identification I'm using to survive your going—now go.* How generous of her to play in this masquerade, if she knew.

16. I spent a certain amount of time that year trying hopelessly to distract my grandmother from the coming loss of her only child—it would mostly wreck her—by pushing my new enthusiasms at her. For instance she and I had a recurrent argument about rock and roll, one which it now strikes me was probably a faint echo, for her, of struggles over my mother's dropping out of Queens College in favor of a Greenwich Village beatnik-folk lifestyle. I worked to find a hit song she couldn't quibble with, and thought I'd found one in Wings' "Mull of Kintyre," which is really just a strummy faux–Irish folk song. I played it for her at top volume and she grimaced, her displeasure not at the music but at the apparent trump card I'd played. Then, on the fade, Paul McCartney gave out a kind *of whoop-whoop* holler and my grandmother seized on this, with relish: "You hear that? He had to go and scream. It wasn't good enough just to sing, he had to scream like an animal!" Her will was too much for me. So when she resisted being dragged to *Star Wars* I probably didn't mind, being uninterested in having her trample on my secret sand castle. She and I were ultimately in a kind of argument about whether or not our family was a site of tragedy, and I probably sensed I was on the losing end of that one.

17. My father lived in a commune for part of that summer, though my mother's illness sometimes drew him back into the house. There was a man in the commune—call him George Lucas—whose married life, which included two young children, was coming apart. George Lucas was the person I knew who'd seen *Star Wars* the most times, apart from me, and we had a ritualized bond over it. He'd ask me how many times I'd seen the film and I'd report, like an emissary with good news from the front. George Lucas had a copy of the soundtrack and we'd sit in the commune's living room and play it on the stereo, which I seem to remember being somewhat unpopular with the commune's larger membership. George Lucas, who played piano and had some classical training, would always proclaim that the score was *really pretty good symphonic composition*—he'd also play me Gustav Holst's *Planets Suite* as a kind of primer, and to show me how the Death Star theme came from Holst's Jupiter—and I would dutifully parrot this for my friends, with great severity: John Williams's score was *really pretty good symphonic composition.*

18. The movie itself, right: of course, I must have enjoyed it immensely the first few times. That's what I least recall. Instead I recall now how as I memorized scenes I fought my impatience, and yet fought not to know I was fighting impatience—all that mattered were the winnowed satisfactions of crucial moments occurring once again, like stations of the cross: "Help me, Obi-Wan Kenobi, you're my only hope," "These aren't the droids you're looking for," "If you strike me down, I'll become more powerful than you can possibly imagine," and the dunk shot of Luke's missiles entering the Death Star's duct. I hated, absolutely, the scene in the Death Star's sewers. I hated Han Solo and Princess Leia's flirtation, after a while, feeling I was being manipulated, that it was too mannered and rote: of course they're grumbling now, that's how it *always* goes. I hated the triumphalist ceremony at the end, though the spiffing-up of the robots was a consolation, a necessary relief. I think I came to hate a lot of

the film, but I couldn't permit myself to know it. I even came, within a year or so, to hate the fact that I'd seen the movie twenty-one times.

19. Why that number? Probably I thought it was safely ridiculous and extreme to get my record into the twenties, yet stopping at only twenty seemed too mechanically round. Adding one more felt plausibly arbitrary, more *realistic.* That was likely all I could stand. Perhaps at twenty-one I'd also attained the symbolic number of adulthood, of maturity. By bringing together *thirteen* and *twenty-one* I'd made *Star Wars* my Bar Mitzvah, a ritual I didn't have and probably could have used that year. Now I was a man.

20. By the time I was fifteen, not only had I long since quit boasting about my love of *Star Wars* but it had become privately crucial to have another favorite movie inscribed in its place. I decided Kubrick's *2001: A Space Odyssey* was a suitably noble and alienated choice, but that in order to make it official I'd have to see it more times than *Star Wars.* An exhausting proposition, but I went right at it. One day at the Thalia on West Ninety-fifth Street I sat alone through *2001* three times in a row in a nearly empty theater, a commitment of some nine hours. That day I brought along a tape recorder in order to whisper notes on this immersion experience to my friend Eliot—I also taped *Also sprach Zarathustra* all six times. If *Star Wars* was my Bar Mitzvah then *2001* was getting laid, an experience requiring a more persuasive maturity, and one which I more honestly enjoyed, especially fifteen or twenty showings in. Oddly enough, though, I never did completely overwrite *Star Wars* with *2001.* Instead I stuck at precisely twenty-one viewings of the second movie as well, leaving the two in a dead heat. Even that number was only attained years later, at the University Theater in Berkeley, California, two days after the 1989 Loma Prieta earthquake. There was a mild aftershock which rumbled the old theater during the Star Gate sequence, a nice touch.

21. I'll never see another film so many times, though I still count. I've seen *The Searchers* twelve times—a cheat, since it was partly research.

Otherwise, I usually peak out at six or seven viewings, as with *Bringing Up Baby* and *Three Women* and *Love Streams* and *Vertigo*, all films I believe I love more than either *Star Wars* or *2001*. But that kid who still can't decide which of the two futuristic epics to let win the struggle for his mortal soul, the kid who left the question hanging, the kid who partly invented himself in the vacuum collision of *Star Wars* and real loss—that kid is me.

Speak, Hoyt-Schermerhorn

Here's where I am: in the subway, but not on a train. I'm standing on one platform, gazing at another. Moaning trains roll in, obscuring my view; I wait for them to pass. The far platform, the one I'm inspecting, isn't lit. The tiles along the abandoned platform's wall are stained—I mean, more than in some ordinary way—and the stairwells are caged and locked, top and bottom. Nothing's happening there, and it's happening round the clock.

I've been haunting this place lately, the Hoyt-Schermerhorn station. But the more time I spend, the further it reels from my grasp. And, increasingly, I'm drawing looks from other passengers on the platforms and upstairs, at the station's mezzanine level. Subway stations—the platforms and stairwells and tunnels, the passages themselves—are sites of deep and willed invisibility. Even the geekiest transit buffs adore the trains, not the stations. By lingering here, I've set off miniature alarms in nearby minds, including my own. I've allied myself with the malingerers not on their way to somewhere else. My investigation of this place reeks of a futility so deep it shades toward horror.

Undercover transit policemen are trained to watch for "loopers —

that is, riders who switch from one train car to the next at each stop. Loopers are understood to be likely pickpockets, worthy of suspicion. Even before that, though, loopers are guilty of using the subway *wrong*. In truth, every subway rider is an undercover officer in a precinct house of the mind, noticing and cataloguing outré and dissident behavior in his fellows even while cultivating the outward indifference for which New Yorkers are famous, above and below ground. It may only be safe to play at not noticing others because our noticing senses are sharpened to trigger-readiness. Jittery subway shooter Bernhard Goetz once ran for mayor. He may not have been electable, but he had a constituency.

As it happens, I'm also an inveterate looper, though I do it less these days. I'll still sometimes loop to place myself at the right exit stairwell, to save steps if I'm running late. I've looped on the 7 train out to Shea Stadium, searching for a friend headed for the same ballgame. More than anything, though, I looped as a teenager, on night trains, looping as prey would, to skirt trouble. I relate this form of looping to other subterranean habits I learned as a terrified child. For instance, a tic of boarding—I'll stand at one spot until a train stops, then abruptly veer left- or right-ward, to enter a car other than the one for which I might have appeared to be waiting. This to shake pursuers, of course. Similarly, a nighttime trick of exiting at lonely subway stations: at arrival I'll stay in my seat until the doors have stood open for a few seconds, then dash from the train. In these tricks my teenager self learned to cash in a small portion of the invisibility that is not only each subway rider's presumed right but his duty to other passengers, whose irritation and panic rises at each sign of oddness, in exchange for tiny likelihoods of increased safety.

By this law of meticulously observed abnormalities, then, my spying here at Hoyt-Schermerhorn goes noticed, triggers a flutter of disapproval in other inhabitants of the station. This may be deserved. I'm not here for a train. I've come seeking something other than a subway ride. What I'm trying to do maybe can't be done: inhabit and understand the Hoyt-Schermerhorn station as a place. Worse, I'm trying to remember it, to restore it to its home in *time*. There's no greater perversity, since a subway station is a sinkhole of destroyed and thwarted time. By standing here trying to remember Hoyt-Schermerhorn I've only triggered its profoundest resistance: I'm using it wrong.

The origins of New York's underground trains, like those of the city itself, reflect a bastard convergence of utopian longing and squalid practicality—land grabs, sweetheart deals, lined pockets. The city's first, thwarted subway was no different: a Jules Verne dream, one instantly snuffed by Tammany Hall, that paradigmatic political machine. The story has the beauty of a Greek myth: a short length of pneumatic subway built in 1869 *in secret* beneath Broadway by a gentleman engineer determined to alleviate the choking daylight nightmare of New York's foot, pig, horse, stagecoach, and surface railway traffic, against the status quo wishes of Tammany's Boss Tweed, who rolled in troughs of money extorted from trolley and omnibus companies. The tube's builder, Alfred Ely Beach, ought to be the hero of one of those elegiac novels of Time Travelers in Olde New York—editor of *Scientific American*, architect of American patent law, he was also a health nut and an opera buff, and the man in whose office Edison first demonstrated the phonograph ("Good morning, Sir . . . How do you like the talking box?"). In fifty-eight nights of covert digging Beach's crew created a 312-foot tunnel, then assembled an elegant wooden, horseshoe-shaped subway car, powered by a giant electric fan. When he unveiled his miracle to the press—in an underground waiting room fitted with curtains, stuffed chairs, painted frescoes, a goldfish fountain and waterfall, grandfather clock, and zircon lamps—his demonstration subway caused a sensation. Tweed, aghast at what had hatched beneath his feet, roused an entrepreneurial assault on Beach's tunnel, investing his capital—and New York's immediate future—in elevated lines rather than subways. The life was squeezed from Beach's dream. His tunnel was rented for wine storage, then forgotten. When in 1912 diggers excavating for the BMT line stumbled unwittingly into Beach's intact waiting room, his drained fountain and extinguished lamps, his stilled wooden car, they must have felt like intruders on Tut's tomb.

When you're a child, everything local is famous. On that principle, Hoyt-Schermerhorn was the most famous subway station in the world. It was the first I knew, and it took years for me to disentangle my primal fascination with its status as a functional ruin, an indifferent home to clockwork chaos, from the fact that it was, in objective measure, an anomalous place. Personal impressions—family stories, and my own—and neighborhood lore swirled in my exaggerated regard. In fact the place was cool and weird beyond my obsession's parameters, cooler and weirder than most subway stations anyway.

My neighborhood, as I knew it in the 1970s, was an awkwardly gentrifying residential zone. The Hoyt-Schermerhorn station stood at the border of the vibrant mercantile chaos of Fulton Street—once the borough's poshest shopping and theater boulevard, it had suffered a steep decline, through the fifties and sixties, from Manhattanesque grandeur to ghetto pedestrian mall. Now no less vital in its way, the place was full of chain outlets and sidewalk vendors, many selling African liquorice-root chews and "Muslim" incense and oils alongside discount socks and hats and mittens. The station itself gave testimony to the lost commercial greatness of the area. Like some Manhattan subway stops, though fewer and fewer every year, it housed businesses on its mezzanine level: a magazine shop, a shoeshine stand, a bakery. Most telling and shrouded at once were the series of ruined shop-display windows that lined the long corridor from the Bond Street entrance. Elegant blue-and-yellow tile work labeled them with an enormous "L"—standing for what, exactly? The ruined dressmakers' dummies and empty display stands behind the cracked glass weren't saying.

The station was synonymous with crime. A neighborhood legend held that Hoyt-Schermerhorn consistently ranked highest in arrests in the whole transit system. Hoyt and Bond streets made vents from the Fulton Mall area, where purse snatchers and street dealers were likely to flee and be cornered. The station also houses one of the borough's three transit police substations, a headquarters for subway cops which legislates over a third of Brooklyn's subway system—so perhaps it was merely that suspects nabbed elsewhere in the system are brought there to register their actual arrest? I've never been able to corroborate the legend. The presence of cops and robbers in the same place has a kind of chicken-and-egg quality. Or should it be considered as a Heisenbergian "observer" problem: Do we arrest you because we see you? Would we arrest you as much elsewhere if we were there?

However ridiculous it may seem, it is true that within sight of that police substation my father, his arms laden with luggage for a flight out of JFK, had his pocket picked while waiting on line for a token. And the pay phone in the station was widely understood to have drug-dealers-only status. Maybe it does still. For my own part I was once detained, not arrested, trying to breeze the wrong way through an exit gate, flashing an imaginary bus pass at the token agent, on my way to high school. A cop gave me a ticket and turned me around to go home and get money for a token. I tried to engage my cop in sophistry: How could I be ticketed for a crime that had been prevented? Shouldn't he let me through to ride the train if I were paying the price for my misdeed? No cigar.

Other peculiarities helped Hoyt-Schermerhorn colonize my dreams. The station featured not only the lively express A train, and its pokey local equivalent, the CC, but also the erratic and desultory GG, a train running a lonely trail through Bedford-Stuyvesant into Queens. The GG—now shortened to the G—was the only subway line in the entire system never to penetrate Manhattan. All roads lead to Rome, but not the GG. Hoyt-Schermerhorn also hosted a quickly abandoned early-eighties transit experiment, "The Train to the Plane"—basically an A train which, for an additional fare, ran an express shot to the airport. For my friends and me, the Train to the Plane was richly comic on several grounds—first of all, because it didn't actually go to the airport: you took a bus from the end of the line. Second, for its twee and hectoring local-television ad—"Take the train to the plane, take the train to the plane," etc. And last because the sight of it, rumbling nearly empty into Hoyt-Schermerhorn with the emblem of an airplane in place of its identifying number or letter, suggested a subway train that was fantasizing itself some other, less inglorious and earthbound conveyance.

The Train to the Plane was younger cousin to a more successful freak train, also run through Hoyt-Schermerhorn: the Aqueduct Special, which took horse-racing bettors out to the track on gambling afternoons. It flourished from 1959 to 1981, when it became a casualty of Off-Track Betting, the walk-in storefront gambling establishments that soon dotted the city. The Aqueduct Special made use of Hoyt-Schermerhorn's strangest feature: its two quiescent tracks and dark spare platform, that parallel ghost—the platform I'd come to gaze at so many years later. As a kid, I took that dark platform for granted. Later, I'd learn how rare it was—though the system contains whole ghost stations, dead to trains, and famously host to homeless populations and vast graffiti master-pieces, no other active station has a ghost platform.

Even if I'd known it, I wasn't then curious enough to consider how those two unused tracks and that eerie platform spoke, as did the ruined display windows, of the zone's dwindled splendor, its former place as a hub. Where I lived was self-evidently marginal to Manhattan—who cared that it was once something grander? What got me excited about Hoyt-Schermerhorn's fourth platform was this: one summer day in 1979 I found a film crew working there, swirling in and out of the station from rows of trucks parked along Schermerhorn Street. Actors costumed as both gang members and as high-school students dressed for prom night worked in a stilled train. The movie, I learned from a bored assistant director standing with a walkie-talkie at one of the subway entrances, was called *The Warriors*. My squalid home turf had been redeemed as pictur-esque. New Yorkers mostly take film crews for granted as an irritant part of the self-congratulatory burden of living in the World Capital. But I was like a hick in my delight at Hoyt-Schermerhorn's moment in the sun. I was only afraid that like a vampire or ghost, the station wouldn't actu-ally be able to be captured in depiction: What were the odds this crappy-looking movie with no movie stars would ever be released? By picking my turf the crew had likely sealed their doom.

I became a regular customer in 1978. That year I began commuting most of the length of Manhattan, a one-hour ride from Brooklyn to 135th Street, to attend Music and Art, a famous public high school. The A train out of Hoyt-Schermerhorn was now my twice-daily passage, to and from. My companion was Lynn Nottage, a kid from the block I grew up on, a street friend. Lynn was from a middle-class black family; I was from a bohemian white one. We had never gone to school together in

Brooklyn—Lynn had been at private school—but now were high-school freshmen together, in distant Harlem. Lynn had the challenge of getting to school on time with me as her albatross. Some mornings the sound of her ringing the doorbell was my alarm clock.

We were students not only of Music and Art but of the A train. Our block felt in many ways like an island in a sea of strife, and Hoyt-Schermerhorn was a place where the sea lapped at the island. Lynn and I had a favorite bum who resided in the station's long passage from the Bond Street entrance, whom Lynn called "Micro-Man," not for his size but for the way his growling complaints boomed in the echo chamber of the station like a microphone. One day Lynn screamed theatrically: she'd spotted a rat behind the smeared glass of the mezzanine-bakery's display counter. I quit buying doughnuts there. Downstairs, we'd fit ourselves into jammed cars, child commuters invisible to the horde. The trip took an hour each way, long enough going in for me to copy the entirety of Lynn's math homework and still read four or five chapters of a paper-back. (I'd read another third or so of each day's book at school, during lunch hour or behind my desk during class, then finish it just as we pulled into Hoyt-Schermerhorn again on the return trip. By this system I read five novels a week for the four years of high school.)

Lynn and I had habits. We stood in a certain spot on the platform, to board the same train every morning (despite an appearance of chaos, the system is regular). Most mornings we rode the same subway car, the conductor's car. Had we been advised to do this by protective parents? I don't know. Anyhow, we became spies, on the adults, the office workers, tourists, beggars, and policemen, who'd share segments of our endless trip. We took a special delight in witnessing the bewilderment of riders trapped after Fifty-ninth Street, thinking they'd boarded a local, faces sagging in defeat as the train skipped every station up to 125th, the longest express hop in the system. Also, we spied on our own conductor. The conductor's wife rode in with him to work—she'd been aboard since somewhere before Hoyt-Schermerhorn—then kissed him goodbye at a stop in the financial district. Two stops later, his girlfriend boarded the train. They'd kiss and moon between stops until she reached her destina-tion. Lynn and I took special pleasure in witnessing this openly, staring like evil Walter Keane kids so the conductor felt the knife-edge of our complicity. Twenty-five years later I'm haunted by that wife.

This was the year another student, a talented violinist, had been pushed from a train platform, her arm severed and reattached. The incident unnerved us to the extent we were able to maintain it as conscious knowledge, which we couldn't and didn't. There were paltry but somehow effective brackets of irony around our sense of the city's dangers. Lynn and I were soon joined by Jeremy and Adam, other kids from Dean Street, and we all four persistently found crime and chaos amusing. The same incidents that drew hand-wringing from our parents and righteous indignation from the tabloids struck us as merry evidence of the fatuousness of grown-ups. Naturally the world sucked, naturally the authorities blinked. Anything was possible. Graffiti was maybe an art form, certainly a definitive statement as to who had actually grasped the nature of reality as well as the workings of the reeling system around you: not adults, but the kids just a year or three older than you, who were scary but legendary. The entire city was like the school in the Ramones' movie *Rock 'n' Roll High School*, or the college in *Animal House*—the dean corrupt and blind, the campus an unpatrolled playground. Our own fear, paradoxically, was more evidence, like the graffiti and the conductor's affair, of the reckless, wide-open nature of this world. It may have appeared from the outside that Lynn and Jeremy and Adam and I were cowering in this lawless place, but in our minds we romped.

The names of the three limbs of the subway—the IRT (Interborough Rapid Transit), the BMT (Brooklyn-Manhattan Transit), and the IND (Independent Subway)—are slowly falling from New Yorkers' common tongue, and the last enamel signs citing the old names will soon be pried off. Slipping into shadow with those names is the tripartite origin of the subway, the fact that each of the three was once a separate and rival corporation. The lines tried to squeeze one another out of business, even as they vied with now-extinct rival forms: streetcars and elevated trains. On this subject, the language of the now-unified system, the official maps and names, has grown mute. But the grammar of the lines and stations themselves, with their overlaps and redundancies, their strange omissions and improvised passageways, still pronounces this history everywhere.

The early subway pioneered in crafty partnership with realtors and developers. Groping for new ridership, owners threw track deep into farmland, anticipating (and creating) neighborhoods like Bensonhurst and Jackson Heights. But the IND, which built and operated Hoyt-Schermerhorn, was a latecomer, an interloper. Unlike its older siblings, the IND clung to population zones, working to siphon excess riders from overloaded lines. The city's destiny wasn't horizontal now, but vertical, perhaps fractal, a break with the American frontier impulse in favor of something more dense and strange.

The new trains running through Hoyt-Schermerhorn quickly mothballed both the Schermerhorn trolley and the old Fulton elevated line— but first the station had to be dug. Construction of new stations in a city webbed with infrastructure was a routine marvel: according to Stan Fischler's *Uptown, Downtown*, tunneling for the IND required, beyond the 22 million cubic yards of rock and earth displaced, and 7 million man-days of labor, the *relocation* of 26 miles of water and gas pipes, 350 miles of electrical wire, and 18 miles of sewage pipes. What's notable in period photographs, though, is the blithe disinterest in the faces of passersby, even at scenes of workers tunneling beneath a street where both a trolley and an el remain in operation. The Sixth Avenue tunnel at Thirty-fourth Street was an engineering marvel in its day, a dig threaded beneath the Broadway BMT subway and over the Pennsylvania Railroad (now Amtrak) tubes, as well as an even-more-deeply buried water main. "The most difficult piece of subway construction ever attempted," is almost impossible to keep in mind on an F train as it slides blandly under Herald Square today.

Alfred Kazin, in *A Walker in the City*, wrote:

> All those first stations in Brooklyn—Clark, Borough Hall, Hoyt, Nevins, the junction of the East and West side express lines—told

me only that I was on the last leg home, though there was always
a stirring of my heart at Hoyt, where the grimy subway platform
was suddenly enlivened by Abraham and Straus's windows of
ladies' wear . . .

When a friend directed me to this passage, thinking he'd solved the mystery of those deserted shop windows in the Hoyt-Schermerhorn passage, I at least had a clue. I searched the corporate history of Abraham and Straus—Brooklyn's dominant department store and a polestar in my childhood constellation of the borough's tarnished majesty, with its brass fixtures and uniformed elevator operators, and the eighth floor's mysterious stamp- and coin-collector's counters. In the A&S annals I found the name of a Fulton Street rival: Frederick Loeser and Company, one of the nation's largest department stores for almost a century, eventually gobbled up by A&S in a merger. The 1950s were to such stores as the Mesozoic was to the dinosaurs—between 1952 and 1957 New York lost Loeser's, Namm's, Wanamaker's, McCreery's, and Hearn's; the names alone are concrete poetry.

I'd nailed my tile-work "L": Loeser's created display windows in the new Hoyt-Schermerhorn station to vie with A&S's famous (at least to Alfred Kazin) windows at Hoyt. Kazin's windows are visible as bricked-in tile window frames today, but like the smashed and dusty Loeser's windows of my childhood, they go ignored. Meanwhile, aboveground on Fulton Street, the name Loeser's has reemerged like an Etch A Sketch filigree on some second-story brickwork, as lost urban names sometimes do.

The abandoned platform was a mystery shallower to penetrate than Loeser's "L." The extra track connects the abandoned platform to an abandoned station, three blocks away on Court Street. This spur of misguided development was put out of its misery in 1946, and sat unused until the early sixties, when the MTA realized it had an ideal facility for renting to film and television crews. The empty station and the curve of track running to the ghost platform at Hoyt-Schermerhorn allowed filmmakers to pull trains in and out of two picturesque stations along a nice curved wall, without disturbing regular operations. The nonpareil among the hundreds of movies made on subway property is the subway-hijacking thriller *The Taking of Pelham One Two Three*. It was in Hoyt-Schermerhorn's tunnel that Robert Shaw and his cohorts stripped off fake mustaches and trench coats and, clutching bags of ransom millions, made their hopeless dash for daylight, and it was in Hoyt-Schermerhorn's tunnel that Shaw, cornered by crusading MTA inspector Walter Matthau, stepped on the third rail and met his doom.

And then there's *The Warriors*. The film is based on a novel by Sol Yurick, itself based on Xenophon's *Anabasis*, an account of a band of Greek mercenaries fighting their way home through enemy turf. Yurick translated Xenophon into New York street gangs; his book is a late and rather lofty entry, steeped in the tone of Camus's *The Stranger*, in the "teen panic" novels of the fifties and sixties. Next, Walter Hill, a director whose paradigm is the Western, turned Yurick's crisp, relentless book into the definitive image of a New York ruled by territorial gangs, each decorated absurdly and ruling their outposts absolutely.

The movie inspired a wave of theater-lobby riots during its theatrical run. It's a cult object now, lauded in hip-hop by Puff Daddy and the Wu-Tang Clan, and cherished by New Yorkers my age, we who preen in our old fears—call us the '77 Blackout Vintage—for mythologizing the crime-ruled New York of the seventies more poignantly, and absurdly, than *Kojak* or *The French Connection*. For, in the film, it is the gang themselves who become the ultimate victims of the city's chaos. In this New York, even the Warriors wish they'd stayed home. For me, a fifteen-year-old dogging the steps of the crew as they filmed, it was only perfect that a fake gang had occupied Hoyt-Schermerhorn's fake platform. The film, etching my own image of the city into legend, began its work even before its public life.

Yurick's book has been reissued again, with a *Warriors* still on the jacket and a long new author's Introduction, detailing the classical and existentialist roots of the novel. Yurick shares his perplexity that this least ambitious of his books should survive on the back of a movie: "There hasn't been one film made in the United States that I would consider see-

ing five times, as many who love the film version of *The Warriors* did."
Years later, I met the wizened Yurick on a train platform, though not the
subway. We disembarked together in Providence, Rhode Island, each a
guest at the same literary conference, and, unknowingly, companion riders on an Amtrak from New York. Our hosts had failed to meet our train,
and as the locals all scattered to their cars, the family members or lovers
to their reunions, we were left to discover one another, and our dilemma.
Yurick shrugged fatalistically—should we have expected better? He
summed his perspective in a sole world-weary suggestion: "Wanna
nosh?"

Michael Lesy's 1973 book, *Wisconsin Death Trip*, is a mosaic of vintage
photographs and newspaper accounts of eccentric behavior and spastic
violence in turn-of-the-century rural Wisconsin. In a flood of miniature
evidence it makes the case that stirring just under the skin of this historical site is mayhem, sexuality, the possibility of despair. The book, a cor-
rective to homilies of a pastoral American countryside, is a catalogue of
unaccountable indigenous lust, grief, revenge, and sudden joy.

Poring over old newspaper clippings that mentioned the station, I
began to imagine my equivalent to Lesy's book: *Hoyt-Schermerhorn
Death Trip*. "TWO ARE KILLED BY POLICE IN GUN BATTLE, 1/23/73: Neither of
the slain men was immediately identified. But the police said that one of
them had been wanted for several bank robberies and for allegedly
shooting at policemen last Wednesday night in the Hoyt-Schermerhorn
Street subway station . . ." "WOMAN HURT IN SUBWAY FALL, 6/19/58: A 55-
year-old woman was critically injured yesterday when she fell or jumped
in front of a southbound IND express train at the Hoyt-Schermerhorn
Street station in Brooklyn . . ." "37 HURT IN CRASH OF TWO IND TRAINS, ONE
RAMS REAR OF ANOTHER IN DOWNTOWN BROOKLYN DURING EVENING RUSH,
7/18/70: . . . there was a rending of metal at the crash, she said, and then
the car tilted. All the lights went out. She said there were sparks and the
car filled with smoke. The girl said she was thrown to the floor and, terrified, began screaming . . ." "STRANGER PUSHES WOMAN TO DEATH UNDER A
TRAIN, 2/2/75: A 25-year-old woman was thrown to her death in front of
an onrushing subway train in Brooklyn yesterday by a man who appar-

ently was a total stranger to her, the police said . . . the incident took place at about 6:15 P.M. in the Hoyt-Schermerhorn IND station, which was crowded with shoppers at the time. According to witnesses, including the motorman, the man suddenly stepped up to the victim, who had her back to him, and pushed her forward in front of the train without saying a word . . ." "400 BOYCOTTING STUDENTS RIOT, HURL BRICKS, BEAT OTHER YOUTHS, 2/18/65: Four hundred boycotting Negro students broke through police barricades outside Board of Education headquarters in Brooklyn yesterday in a brick-throwing, window-breaking riot . . . The disturbances spread over a two-mile area and onto subway trains and stations . . . A group of 60 youths attacked a group of six white students on the Clinton-IND's GG line . . . They were apprehended at the Hoyt-Schermerhorn Station by 15 transit policemen . . ." "300 IN SUBWAY HELP TILT CAR AND RELEASE BOY'S WEDGED FOOT, 9/2/70: A rescue team of subway passengers, hastily organized by three transit policemen, tipped back a 54-ton subway car last night to free an 11-year-old boy whose foot was wedged between the car and the platform at a downtown Brooklyn station . . . The boy . . . was running for an IND A train when his leg was caught between the platform and train at the Hoyt-Schermerhorn station."

Contemplation of the life of a site like Hoyt-Schermerhorn becomes, in the end, tidal. The lapping of human moments forms a pulse or current, like the lapping of trains through the underground tunnels, or like the Doppler-effect fading of the certain memories from the planet, as they're recalled for the penultimate time, and then the last: When will the last person to have purchased panty hose or a razor at Loeser's or Namm's pass from the earth? When will the last of those three hundred who rocked the train car off the boy's pinned leg, or the last of those four hundred Negro boycotters, be gone?

A white kid raised inside the liberal sentiments of a middle-class family yet living in an area fringed with crime and poverty met a choice. It was possible to identify with and assimilate to the harsher truths of the street, and so toughen, somewhat, to fear. Alternately, a kid could carry his parents' sensitivities, and standards, with him, out-of-doors. The price was obvious. Most of us, whether we ended in one camp or another, wavered. I was a "good" kid, and a bullied one, yet I recall dozens of moments when I slid briefly across the separation line. Once, on a basketball court, I allowed myself to meld into a crowd of Puerto Rican kids, with whom I'd been playing, as they briefly halted the game to harass and threaten a single Asian man, a gay man, off a neighboring court. I wasn't violent; the incident hardly was. But the man was the boyfriend of a pal of my mother's, and I'd been a guest in their elegant town house. When my mother's friend, a gay man considerably huskier than his young lover, returned to the court with a baseball bat and, bellowing, sent us scurrying from our game, his eyes met mine and I was disgraced, wrenched between concurrent selves.

The moment was precursor to a worse one. This was the summer between high school and college, which is to say the verge of my escape from Brooklyn for the first time. I've come to understand how fraught that moment was for me, as I considered or refused to consider what I was involuntarily carrying with me out of my childhood environment. My girlfriend was from upstate New York, but lived in my city, my neighborhood, for that summer before we both embarked to college. She worked nights as a waitress in Manhattan and rode the A train in and out of Hoyt-Schermerhorn. She was frightened, as she perhaps should have been, to walk the several blocks home from that station after eleven, and so I'd promised always to meet her. I often lightly mocked her fear—but that bit of overcompensation, lousy as it sounds, wasn't my crime.

My crime was this: one night, going to the station to pick her up, I impulsively waited in shadow by the entrance instead of making myself visible. I had no plan. I was fooling around. She paused and looked for me, just for a moment, plainly afraid to stand there waiting alone, as she absolutely should have been: it was a different thing to walk swiftly home than it was to linger. I could have stepped forward easily, but instead, frozen in my stupid jape, I only watched her. And then, as she began walking home without me, I followed.

I was certain she'd turn and see me, and that it would be oddly funny, but she never did. She was afraid to turn to see whose footsteps followed her, of course. I trailed her home, compounding my mistake with each accelerating footstep, until I at last overtook her just outside the door. While I tried to explain, she trembled, in fear which converted immediately, and rightly, to rage. Denial has covered any recollection of my words by now, but I know they were hopelessly inadequate to repair what I'd told myself was a harmless joke—though I was walking behind her I'd still been protecting her, hadn't I?—and was actually such a cruel joke it wasn't a joke at all. I'd hardly claim to be Patty Hearst, but there was a touch of the Stockholm syndrome in my behavior. I was bestowing on another a trace, or more than a trace, of the fear I'd absorbed for years.

The glamour of Abraham and Straus, for so long the one survivor among Brooklyn's great stores, has evaporated. A&S's carcass houses a Macy's now, with a small plaque on its Hoyt Street side commemorating the history of A&S, if you want to seek it out. Me, I don't have the heart to go inside the Macy's to see what remains of A&S's Art Deco elevators—let it remain the place where I first met Santa, where I used to buy wheat-backed pennies to fill out holes in my penny collection, and thousand-piece jigsaw puzzles.

Not that those memories would likely be diminished by a visit. Perhaps, instead, I'm afraid of their intensification. Every time I pass through Hoyt-Schermerhorn's Bond Street corridor, past Loeser's tile "L" and bricked-up windows, I recall the first time I saw them, and the start of my lifelong romance, a New Yorker's typical romance with our limitless secret neighborhood, the one running beneath all the others. This was my first subway memory, here: the passage, those windows. Nothing subsequent, not thousands of high-school days, not *The Warriors* nor my own feeble crimes, can displace this memory's primacy, or fade its color. I held my mother's hand. I was being taken to her office, in Manhattan. Perhaps it was a day off from school, I don't know. I rode the subway for the first time I can recall, but I don't remember the train. I remember the station.

Identifying with Your Parents,

or

The Return of the King

"I dreamt last night that I'd write this essay in panels of prose, mimicking the style of a comic book, in which meaning lurks in the gaps between, Sue!"

"But Reed, what about the *baby*?!?"

In the mid-seventies I had two friends who were into Marvel Comics. Karl, whose parents were divorced, and Luke, whose parents were among the most stable I knew. My parents were something in between: separated, or separating, sometimes living together and sometimes apart, and each of them with lovers.

I would never have been able to name that difference in 1975, however, let alone account for how it felt. The difference I understood was this: Luke had an older brother, Peter, whom both Luke and I idealized in absentia. Peter had left behind a collection of sixties Marvel comic books, in sacrosanct box files. These included a nearly complete run of *The Fantastic Four*, the famous 102 issues drawn by Jack Kirby and scripted by Stan Lee, a defining artifact (I now know) of the "Silver Age of Comics."

Luke was precocious, worldly, full of a satirical brilliance I didn't always understand but pretended to, as I pretended to understand his frequent references to "Aunt Petunia" and the "Negative Zone" and the "Baxter Building." He was disdainful of childish pursuits and disdainful of my early curiosity about sex (I didn't catch the contradiction in this until later).

Luke didn't buy new comics so much as he read and reread old ones. Luke's favorite comic-book artist was Jack Kirby.

Karl was precocious, secretive, and rebellious, full of intimations of fireworks and drugs and petty thievery that frightened and thrilled me. He was curious about sex, and unaware of or uninterested in the early history of Marvel superheroes. For him Marvel began with the hip, outsiderish loner heroes of the seventies—Ghost Rider, Luke Cage, Warlock, Iron Fist. His favorite comic-book artist was John Byrne.

Karl got in trouble a lot. Luke didn't.

Though all three of us lived in rough parts of Brooklyn, Karl and I went to public school together, close to a housing project, while Luke went to Saint Ann's School, safe in moneyed Brooklyn Heights. It was this, I'm certain, that tipped my allegiance to Karl in those years. Karl and I, in our school days, had been forced to adopt a stance of endurance and shame together, a Kabuki of cringing postures in response to a world of systematic bullying. That was a situation I could no more have explained to Luke than to my parents. Karl and I never discussed it either, but we knew it was shared.

In 1976 Marvel announced, with what seemed to Karl and me great fanfare, the return of Jack Kirby, the "King" of Comics, as an artist-writer—a full "auteur"—on a series of Marvel titles. The announcement wasn't a question of press conferences, mind you, or advertisements in other media, only sensational reports on the Bullpen Bulletins pages of Marvel Comics themselves, the CNN of our little befogged minds at the time. Kirby was the famed creator or co-creator of a vast collection of classic Marvel characters: the Fantastic Four, the Hulk, Thor, Silver Surfer, Doctor Doom, the Inhumans. In a shadowy earlier career (as captives within the Marvel hype machine, Karl and I had bought into a view that nothing really existed before 1962) Kirby was also the creator of Captain America—his career reached into what was for us the prehistory of comics. The notion that he was about to reclaim his territory was rich and disturbing. In fact, what he would turn out to bring to Marvel was a paradoxical combination: clunkily old-fashioned virtues that had been outmoded, if not surpassed, by subsequent Marvel artists, together with a baroque and nearly opaque futuristic sensibility that would leave most readers chilled, largely alienated from what he was trying to do. Later I'd learn that Kirby's return created rifts in the ranks of the younger Marvel writers and artists, who resented the creative autonomy he'd been granted and found the results laughable. At the time all I knew was that Kirby's return created a rift between myself and Karl.

Kirby hadn't been inactive in the interlude between his classic sixties work for Marvel and his mid-seventies return. He'd been in exile at DC, Marvel's older, more august and square rival. In the sixties, DC, despite its stewardship of Batman and Superman, had lost much ground to Marvel—due to Kirby and Lee's great creations, of course. Then, after Kirby's relationship with Stan Lee had become aggrieved, DC plucked him away, and handed him, for a while, full creative control of an epic series of Kirby-created titles called *The New Gods*. In doing so, they'd gotten more, and other, than they'd bargained for—*The New Gods* comics were massively ambitious, and massively arcane. Though acclaimed by some as masterworks, they never found much traction with the readership. The reason for their commercial failure is pretty specific. The comics were hard to relate to. While Kirby's most "cosmic" creations at Marvel—Galactus, the Silver Surfer, the Inhumans, etc.—were always bound to human-scale stories by their relationships to prosaic earthly characters—that is, for the most part, the homely and squabbling Fantastic Four themselves—at DC he created a pantheon of gods but didn't bother with the humans. Similarly, at Marvel his all-powerful monster-strongman types—Hulk, Thing, and, in another sense, Thor—all had fragile human identities to protect or mourn. At DC, Kirby seemed to have flown off into his own cosmic realms of superheroes and supervillains without any important human counterparts or identities. The feet of his work never touched the ground. The results were impressive, and quite boring.

What he unveiled on his return to Marvel was more of the very same, in two new venues: *The Eternals*, which introduced another dualistic pantheon of battling gods, and *2001*, ostensibly based on Kubrick's film. Each of these series indulged Kirby's most abstracted work in his most high-flown cosmic register. Each introduced dozens of colorful but remote characters, and each abandoned or distended traditional story-telling to such a degree that the audience—I mean me and Karl—was mostly baffled.

But if   And
This were   a
Drawn by   part
Kirby in   of
The 1970s   me
It would   aches
Be a Massive   to
Gleaming   reveal
Hysterically   to
Hyper-articulated   you
Psychedelic   that
Edifice of   daunting
Mechanistic   inhuman
Prose   spectacle
Adrift   in
In   Kirby's
Space!   honor!

Studying Jack Kirby now, I'm bewildered that one man can encompass such contradictory things. By contradictory I don't mean his diversity of accomplishments in so many different eras of comics history—his creation, with Joe Simon, of the patriotic anti-Nazi type of superhero in Captain America; his creation, also with Simon, of the basic mold for the "romance" comic; his dominance in the "movie-monster" style of comics that preceded the explosion of inventions at Marvel; that selfsame explosion, which includes at least a share in the invention of both the "star" supervillain (Doctor Doom) and the ambivalent antiheroic type (whether craggily pathetic à la the Hulk or handsomely tormented à la Silver Surfer and Black Bolt); the psychedelic majesty (however thwarted) of the New Gods work at DC. Those aren't contradictory, only boggling in the sense that the accomplishments of a Picasso or a Dylan or a Shakespeare are boggling. By contradictory I mean the fact that in that DC work and then especially in the return to Marvel, Jack Kirby, the greatest innovator in the history of comics, gradually turned into a kind of primitivist genius, disdained as incompetent by much of the audience, but revered by a cult of aficionados somewhat in the manner of an "outsider artist." As his work spun off into abstraction, his human bodies more and more machinelike, his machines more and more molecular and atomic (when they didn't resemble vast sculptures of mouse-gnawed cheese), Kirby became greatly awful, a kind of disastrous genius uncontainable in the form he himself had innovated. It's as though Picasso had, after 1950, become Adolf Wolfli, or John Ford had ended up as John Cassavetes. Or if Robert Crumb turned into his obsessive mad-genius brother, Charles Crumb. Or if Chuck Berry evolved into Sun Ra.

Speaking of Chuck Berry, there's something about my childhood that I've never been able to explain, but I want to attempt to now. I suffered a kind of nerdish fever for authenticity and origins of all kinds, one which led me into some very strange cultural places. The notion of "influence" compelled me, at irrational depths of my being. Any time I heard mention that, say, David Bowie was only really imitating Anthony Newley, I immediately lost interest in David Bowie and went looking for the source, sometimes with the pitiable results that the example suggests. So I was always moving backward through time, and though I was born in 1964 and came to cultural consciousness some time around 1970 or 1971, I particularly adored the culture of the fifties and early sixties: Ernie Kovacs, *The Twilight Zone*, the British Invasion, Lenny Bruce, the Beat writers, film noir, etc. I tended to identify with my parents' taste in things, and with the tastes of my parents' friends, more than with the supposed cultural tokens of my own generation. It was with Luke, in fact, that I went to see a Ralph Bakshi film called *Heavy Traffic*, which contains an unforgettable animated sequence that accompanies and illustrates with crude (and porny) drawings the Chuck Berry song "Maybelline." Thanks to the film I fell in love with Chuck Berry, and while every kid in freshman year of high school was defining their identity according to whether they liked (A) Jimi Hendrix and Pink Floyd and the Doors or (B) the Clash and the Specials and Bad Brains or (C) Cheap Trick and the Cars and Blondie, I was looking into (Z) Chuck Berry and Bo Diddley. It's a commonplace, of course, that we seventies kids were doomed to glance backward, out of our impoverished world of Paul McCartney and Wings, to the era of the Beatles—but I was the only twelve-year-old I've ever known who got into an extended argument with his own mother about whether the Beatles were better before or after *Sgt. Pepper*—my mother on the side of "I Am the Walrus," me on the side of "Drive My Car."

I identified with my parents in other, murkier, and more emotional ways, of course. Not that those are separable from the cultural stuff. Put simply, I was in fearful denial of my own childish neediness. I wished to be an adult in order to be forever spared sympathy or condescension, which reminded me too starkly of my helplessness.

At the moment in my childhood I'm describing now, bodies were beginning to change, and the exact degree and nature of their changes provided psychological opportunities, and thwarted others. Karl at thirteen grew tall, handsome, and dangerously effective at cutting an adult profile. Luke and I each stayed, for the moment, small and childlike.

Karl identified, as I've said, with Marvel's existential loners: the Vision, Warlock, Ghost Rider, etc. By becoming tall and rebellious—he'd begun to write graffiti, smoke pot, fail in school, all pursuits I'd only barely flirted with—he'd eluded childishness by a bodily rejection of it, and by rejecting obedience. The cost was exile from continuity with what was attractive in our parents' worlds, of course. That cost didn't impress Karl, not at that moment anyway.

So here was how, for a time, I tilted back to Luke: he and I were partnered in a more baroque strategy, of rejecting childishness by identifying with our parents, and by sneering at rebellion as childish. As paltry new teenagers we adopted a "you can't fire me, I quit" position.

But Marvel was implicated in my yearning backward—ours, I should say: mine, Luke's, even Karl's. By the time of Kirby's return, the comics-world discourse around Marvel's greatness was explicitly nostalgic. Any counterargument, based on a typically American myth of progress, that our contemporary comics might be even more wonderful, was everywhere undermined by a pining for the heyday of the sixties. This was accomplished most prominently in Stan Lee's two enormously popular trade paperbacks: *Origins* and *Son of Origins*, which reproduced and burnished the creation myths of the great sixties characters. The odor of grandeur, not to mention sanctimony, that clung to any discussion of the Silver Age boom was impossible to clear from one's nostrils after reading the Origins books. There wasn't any way to imagine that the first issues of *Iron Fist* or *Deathlok the Demolisher* would ever be collected in equally biblical compendia. Nostalgia was further propagated in Marvel's reprint titles: *Marvel Tales*, which offered rewarmed *Spider-Man*s, and the too-aptly-titled *Marvel's Greatest Comics*, which put forward—you guessed it—the Kirby-Lee run of *Fantastic Four*s. This was somewhat akin to Paul McCartney and Wings playing covers of Beatles songs on *Wings over America*. We seventies kids couldn't have been issued a clearer message: we'd missed the party.

Speaking of the Beatles (that is, famous sixties culture breakups and their seventies legacies), I ought to give at least a moment to the whole question of the Lee-Kirby authorship controversy. In a nutshell, in the

Origins books, Lee notoriously undersold the contributions of his artist collaborators—that is to say, mostly Kirby, but also Steve Ditko, the penciler of Spider-Man and Doctor Strange. Later, in a dispute over the ownership of Kirby's artwork—the actual drawn pages—Kirby was given extensive chances to play a grouchy old David against Marvel's corporate Goliath, and the comics world rallied around him. He also made public claim to being the sole author of the great characters that had made the Kirby-Lee partnership famous: the Fantastic Four and all their sublime villains and supporting cast, Hulk, Thor, Silver Surfer, etc. (He even once threw in Spider-Man for good measure.) Lee and Kirby *were* a kind of Lennon-McCartney partnership, in several senses: Kirby, like Lennon, the raw visionary, with Lee, like McCartney, providing sweetness and polish, as well as a sense that the audience's hunger for "hooks"—in the form of soap-operatic situations involving romance and family drama, young human characters with ungodlike flaws, gently humorous asides, etc.—shouldn't be undernourished. And, after the breakup, it was Kirby, like Lennon, whom the audience tended to want to credit as the greater genius, and Lee, like McCartney, who took on an aura of the shallow and crafty businessman.

Whoever deserves the lion's share of credit for "inventing" (that is, designing outfits and powers, creating the origin myths and distinctive personae) of the Marvel Silver Age characters, it is unmistakable that in Marvel's greatest comics—I mean, in the *Fantastic Four* issues which were reprinted in *Marvel's Greatest Comics*, the originals of which Luke's brother had assembled—Kirby and Lee were full collaborators who, like Lennon and McCartney, really were more than the sum of their parts, and who derived their greatness from the push and pull of incompatible visions. Kirby always wanted to drag the Four into the Negative Zone—deeper into psychedelic science fiction and existential alienation—while Lee, in his scripting, resolutely pulled them back into the morass of human lives, *hormonal* alienation, teenage dating problems and pregnancy and unfulfilled longings to be human and normal and loved and not to have the Baxter Building repossessed by the city of New York.

Kirby threw at the Four an endless series of ponderous fallen gods, or whole tribes of alienated antiheroes with problems no mortal could credibly contemplate: Galactus and the Silver Surfer, the Inhumans, Doctor Doom, etc. Lee made certain the Four were always answerable to the female priorities of Sue Storm, the Invisible Girl, Reed Richards's wife and famously "the weakest member of the Fantastic Four." She wanted a home for their boy, Franklin; she wanted Reed to stay out of the Negative Zone; and she was willing to quit the Four and quit the marriage to stand up for what she believed.

I seriously doubt whether any seventies Marvel-loving boy ever spared a dram of sexual fantasizing on Sue Storm. We had Valkyrie, Red Sonja, the Cat, Ms. Marvel, Jean Grey, Mantis, and innumerable others available for that. We (I mean, *I*) especially liked the Cat. Sue Storm was, to our conscious minds, truly invisible. She was a parent, a mom calling you home from where you played in the street, telling you it was time to brush your teeth. Not that she wasn't a hottie, but Kirby exalted her beauty in family-album style portraits, showing her nobly pregnant, in a housedress that covered her clavicle. The writers and artists who took over the Fantastic Four after Kirby and, later, Lee departed the series, seemed impatient with the squareness of Sue and Reed's domestic situations. Surely these weren't the hippest of the Kirby-Lee creations. Nevertheless, if you (I mean, *I*) accept my (own) premise (and why shouldn't I?) that the mid- to late-sixties Fantastic Four were the exemplary specimens, the veritable *Rubber Soul* and *Revolver* and *White Album* of comics, and if you further grant that pulling against the tide of all of Kirby's Inhuman Galactacism, that whole army of aliens and gods, was one single character, our squeaky little Sue, then I wonder: Was the Invisible Girl the most important superhero of the Silver Age of Comics?

I'm breaking down here. The royal *we* and the presumptive *you* aren't going to cut it. This is a closed circuit, me and the comics which I read and which read me, and the reading of which by one another, me and the comics, I am now attempting to read, or reread. The fact is I'm dealing with a realm of masturbation, of personal arcana. Stan Lee's rhetoric of community was a weird vibrant lie: every single *true believer*, every single member of the Make Mine Marvel society or whatever the fuck we were meant to be called, received the comics as a private communion with our own obscure and shameful yearnings, and it was miraculous and pornographic to so much as breathe of it to another boy, let alone be initiated by one more knowing. *We* and *you* don't know a thing about what *I* felt back then, any more than *I* know a thing about what *you* felt.

Specifically, nobody much cherishes the comics of Kirby's "return to Marvel" period—*2001, The Eternals, Mister Machine.* Even for souls who take these things all too seriously, those comics have a minor place in the history, defining only an awkward misstep in a dull era at Marvel, before the brief popular renaissance signaled by the ascent of the Chris Claremont *X-Men.* Here, joining the chorus of the indifferent, is Kirby himself, from an interview with Gary Groth of *Comics Journal,* one which ranged over his whole glorious career:

Interviewer: "It always seemed like your last stint at Marvel was a little halfhearted."

Kirby: "Yeah."

Anyway I want to withdraw the Lennon-McCartney comparison, because there's something else I've sensed about the Kirby-Lee partnership: it seems to me that Kirby must have been a kind of ambivalent father figure to Lee. Kirby was only five years older, but they were crucial years—crucial in defining two different types of American manhood. Kirby came of age in the thirties, was toughened by his Depression boyhood and perhaps privately, stoically scarred by his frontline experiences in World War II. Lee seems more like the subsequent kind of American male, the coddled fifties striver who lived in the world his parents had fought for and earned. Lee was more a wannabe beatnik—Maynard G. Krebs, let's say. This difference perhaps underlies the extremes of their contribution to the Fantastic Four: Kirby concerned himself with a clash of dark and light powers, and passionately identified with alien warrior-freaks who, like John Wayne in *The Searchers*, were sworn to protect the vulnerable civilian (or human) societies they were forever incapable of living among. His vision was darkly paternal. Lee was the voice of the teenage nonconformist, looking for kicks in a boring suburb, diffident about the familial structures by which he was nevertheless completely defined.

John Wayne in *The Searchers* is, crucially, a Civil War veteran, made strong and ruined by what he'd glimpsed on the battlefield. Similarly, the first thing to know, and the easiest thing to overlook, about the iconic hard-boiled detective of the Raymond Chandler–Dashiell Hammett–Humphrey Bogart type is that he wears a *trench* coat—that is, he's a veteran of the First World War. I was once told by a biographer who'd researched Jimmy Stewart's years as an air commander in World War II that the crucial material in Stewart's war record was sealed. (Stewart, unlike others who served less vitally but wore their experiences on their sleeves, tended not to talk about the war.) The biographer wondered if Stewart might actually have led a portion of the raid on Dresden, and been protected from infamy by his government. The biographer also wondered if whatever was sealed inside that war record had fueled the deepening and darkening of Stewart's postwar work—the alienation and morbidity and even cynicism that the great and formerly gentle leading man displayed in films like *Vertigo*, *The Naked Spur*, and *Anatomy of a Murder*. Now, when I consider the steady alienation from humankind of Kirby's bands of outsiders—from the Fantastic Four to the Inhumans to the New Gods to the Eternals—I wonder if he might be one of those who could never completely come home again.

But he did try to come home in 1976, to Marvel. And Karl and I bought the hype, and bought the comics. And Karl didn't like them, and I did. Or, anyway, I defended them. I pretended to like them. Karl immediately took up a view, one I've now learned, in my research, was typical of a young seventies Marvel fan: he said Kirby sucked because he didn't draw the human body right. Karl was embarrassed by the clunkiness, the raw and ragged dynamism, the lack of fingernails or other fine detail. Artists like Neal Adams and Gil Kane had, since Kirby, set new standards for anatomical and proportional "realism," and those standards had soon been made peculiarly normative by (to me, much less interesting) artists like John Byrne and George Perez: superhero comics weren't supposed to look "cartoonish" anymore. Karl had no tolerance. I, schooled both in my father's expressionist-painter's love of exaggeration and fantasy, and in Luke's scholarly and tendentious devotion to his older brother's comics, decided I saw what Karl couldn't.

Of course, in my defense of Kirby I was conflating comic art and comic writing. I need to quit conflating them here. That is to say, it's possible to debate the moment in the seventies when Kirby's penciling began to go south. He was good; he got worse. What's undebatable is the execrable, insufferable pomposities of Kirby's dialogue writing in the Marvel work without Lee. Or the deprivations involved in trying to love his galactically distant and rather depressed story lines. As a scripter, as opposed to "idea man," he stunk.

I did try to love the story lines. It mattered to me. With Luke's help I'd understood that Kirby represented our parents' values, the Chuck Berry values. In Kirby resided the higher morality of the Original Creator. That which I'd sworn to uphold, against the shallow killing-the-father imperatives of youth.

Luke, it should be said, never cared about Kirby's return. Luke was a classicist, and didn't buy new comics. I was on my own, hung out to dry by *The Eternals.*

Karl and I were also drawing comics in those days. Well not really comics—we were drawing superheroes: on single pages we'd design a character, detail his costume and powers and affect, then speculate on his adventures. I was profligate in this art, quickly generating a large stack of characters, whose names, apart from "Poison Ivy" and "The Hurler," I can no longer retrieve from the memory hole. Karl drew fewer characters, more carefully, and imparted to them more substantial personalities and histories. One day in Karl's room he and I were arguing about Kirby (we really did this: argue about Kirby) and I formulated a rhetorical question, meant to shock Karl into recognition of Kirby's awesome gifts: Who, I asked Karl, besides Kirby, had ever shown the ability to generate so many characters, so many distinctive costumes, so many different archetypal personas? In reply, Karl turned the tables on me, with a weird trick of undercutting flattery. He said, *You.*

At the time my ego chose to be buoyed by Karl's remark. But really he'd keyed on an increasing childishness in Kirby. None of Kirby's army of new characters at Marvel were ever going to be real, were ever going to mean much to anyone. They weren't fated to live in meaningful stories. They werc only empty costumes, like my own drawings. There was something regressive about Kirby now—he'd become self-affirming, the outsider artist decorating the walls of private rooms.

The comics Karl and I actually relished in 1976 and 1977, if we were honest (and Karl was more honest than me), were *The Defenders*, *Omega the Unknown*, and *Howard the Duck*, all written by a mad genius named Steve Gerber, and *Captain Marvel* and *Warlock*, both written and drawn by another auteur briefly in fashion, named Jim Starlin. As far as the art went, Gerber liked to collaborate with plodding but inoffensive pencilers like Jim Mooney and Sal ("The Lesser") Buscema. Those guys moved the story along well enough. Starlin's were drawn in a slickly hip and mildly psychedelic style exaggerated in the direction of adult comix like *Heavy Metal*, but with the "realistic" musculature that the moment (and Karl) demanded, rather than the Franz Kline kneecaps and biceps of Jack Kirby. Gerber's tales were wordy, satirical and self-questioning, and stuffed full of homely human characters dealing with day-to-day situations: bag ladies, disc jockeys, superheroines' jealous husbands, kids who faced bullying at their local public schools. His approach to the superhero mythos was explicitly deflationary. Starlin was more into wish-fulfillment fantasies of cosmic power, but he was droll and readable, and the scrupulous way he drew his psychedelia was actually indebted (I see now, paging through the stuff) to Steve Ditko's early version of *Doctor Strange*. Enough: I fear I'm losing you. The point is, Gerber and Starlin were the two creators whose work was pitted in the day-to-day contest against "The Return of the King," and they were winning, hands down, even in my muddled and ideological heart.

Local ironies: the alienated, noble, loner type that Karl responded to most of all—embodied for him in Warlock and the Vision, Karl's absolute favorites—was plainly a distillation of pure Kirby characters like the Silver Surfer and Black Bolt. But I couldn't lead Karl to appreciate—why should he have?—Kirby's authorship.

And: Steve Gerber, who in his postmodernish anti-sagas seemed to us utterly our "contemporary" (I have to put that in quotes so that you don't think we literally believed Steve Gerber was fourteen years old), was engaged in a *killing-the-father* imperative of his own, one that leapfrogged over the Silver Age, and also right over my and Karl's heads at the time. That's to say, reading Gerber now, I see that three of his best characters were sly parodies of mid-century comics which Gerber must have grown up reading. Omega the Unknown, a handsome blue-costumed and -haired humanoid from a destroyed planet, and with a kinship with a human boy, was Gerber's undermining of both Superman and the original Captain Marvel (known to us only as the pathetic replicant Shazam). *The Defenders'* Nighthawk, a powerless millionaire with a utility belt and a flying cape, was basically a Batman parody. And Howard was a corrupted Disney duck.

The moment I'm describing would come to a precipitous end. Karl and I were in intermediate school in Brooklyn together until the summer of 1977. Though our friendship was strained toward the end of that time, both by Karl's physical maturation and by the increasing distance between his rebellious nonconformity with the adult world and my parent-identifying nonconformity with the teenage world, we certainly continued to sporadically buy and evaluate Marvel comics together until the end of eighth grade.

It was high school which severed our connection, for what would become years. I went off to Music and Art, in Manhattan, a place much populated by dreamy nerds like myself, and perfectly formulated to indulge my yearning to skip past teenagerhood straight to an adult life: many of my best friends in high school were my teachers. Karl was destined for Stuyvesant High, where he drifted into truancy. Then he'd land at one of our local public high schools, John Jay, where he'd be forced to continue battling a world of bullying I'd left behind.

Luke, meanwhile, was still safe in the preserve of private school, where his negotiation with the call of teenagerhood, and beyond, might be subject to the push and pull of peer pressure, but better isolated from the starkness of the bankrupt city around us. Our friendship, mine and Luke's, was restored somewhat during those high-school years, though I suspect I sometimes eluded him. My public-school experiences had made me worldly in ways that Luke's stubborn cognition, and the advantage of his older brother's influence, couldn't quite match. As for physical maturation, I now shot ahead, to catch up with Karl (though he wasn't around for me to make the comparison), while Luke still lagged slightly. Now, I think, I was to Luke as Karl had been to me; I was his Karl. No rebel, I had nonetheless begun to smoke pot, which Luke still distrusted. No whiz with girls, I was at least comfortable with my puppyish interest, while Luke remained, for the time being, gnarled up regarding that subject.

Between me and Luke, Jack Kirby was still a tacit God, but only on the strength of his canonical sixties work. Luke and I, righteous in our reverence for origins, didn't between us acknowledge Kirby's continued existence. It would have been unseemly, like dwelling on the fact that Chuck Berry, rock 'n' roll's progenitor, had had a seventies novelty hit called "My Ding-a-Ling."

Whether Karl continued to buy comics I couldn't know. And what of the place where our argument about Kirby had been left, in the end? That was lost, along with much else, in the denial surrounding the state of our friendship, which had attenuated to an occasional "hello" on the streets of the neighborhood.

If my own writing   the   manner   would have to
Were to tip over   of a seventies   devolve into
Into abstraction   Kirby comic   an endlessly
And autism in   I suppose it   distended

Sequence of
    less and less
        credible or even
            charming analogies
                and equations until
                    it dropped off the
                        table of our universe
                            into the mad
                                and self-ratifying
                        F A T U O U S   Z O N E!

And there it would spiral forever, oblivious to contempt:

                        Kirby
                                Equals
                                Chuck Berry
            Equals, god help me   Equals
                Sue Storm   I don't know,   John Lennon
            Equals   um,   Equals
            Paul McCartney   Anthony Newley?   Father
        Equals   (or, Jonathan?)   Equals
            Stan Lee   Luke
            Equals   Equals
                Maynard G. Krebs   John Wayne
                Equals   Equals
                    Pink Floyd   Black Bolt
                        Equals   Equals
                        Karl

The last year of high school, before college changed everything, Luke and
I still drifted together occasionally. Now it was he and I who drew

comics—not innocently wishful superheroes, but what we imagined were stark satires, modeled on the work of R. Crumb and other heroes of the "underground." Luke had by then begun dating girls too, and one of our last collaborative productions was a Kirby parody called "Girlfriends from the Earth's Core." A two-page strip, it reworked the material of a failed double date of a month before, when Luke and I had taken two girls, soon to be our first bitter exes, to a fleabag movie theater at the Fulton Mall. Luke "penciled" the pages, and I was the "inker"—I specialized in Kirbyesque polka dots of energy, which we showed rising from the volcanic bodies of the two primordial girlfriends.

I know them both, Luke and Karl. Luke and his wife live in a New England town. The oldest of their children is named Harpo, which strikes me now as more of the reverence for our parents' culture that always drew us together. Luke works making animated films (as Kirby once attempted to, when his comics career was demoralized by the failed return to Marvel). His conversation still features Fantastic Four–derived phrases like "Aunt Petunia" and "It's Clobberin' Time." Kirby is in Luke's DNA; I see it flashing in his eyes. I know for him it is more real than it ever was for me, as real as an older brother who'd slipped out of the house and left Kirby as his placeholder.

Me, I'm a fake, my Kirby-love cobbled from Luke's certainty, Karl's resistance, and Stan Lee's cheerleading. My version of an older brother was Karl, and Karl wasn't reverent about Kirby. Karl was only curious— Kirby was merely on the menu of the possible, alongside Starlin and Gerber, alongside Ghost Rider and Warlock, alongside forgetting about comics and getting into girls or music or drugs instead. Karl never had that kind of crush on his own or other kids' parents—a crush on the books on their shelves, on the records in their collections.

Karl, though, still lives in the Brooklyn neighborhood to which I've returned, and which he never left. He lives down the street, and we're both only a few blocks from the once-treacherous precinct of our shared school. Last week I had him over, and we dug out a box of Marvel comic books. These were the same copies we'd cherished together in 1976 and 1977—for, in an act surely loaded with unexamined rage, I'd purchased Karl's comic collection from him late in our high-school years, when his interest drifted, when our friendship was at its lowest ebb.

Karl isn't urgent about contemplating our old comics, but he's willing. This day, while we were browsing the Kirbys of the Return era, he corrected my memory in a few specifics. Most crucially, he raised the possibility that the argument about Kirby, which had seemed to me loaded with the direst intimations of the choices we were about to make, the failures of good faith with our childhood selves we were about to suffer, had mostly been conducted in my own head. It was when I put a stack of Kirby's *2001*'s in his hands.

"I really got into some of these issues," he said. I could see his features animate with recollection as he browsed Kirby's panels, something impossible to fake even if you had a reason to do so. "I remember this comic book really blew my mind."

"I thought you never liked Kirby," I said feebly, still stuck on my thesis.

"No, I remember when he first came back I was a little slow to get it," Karl told me, after I'd explained what I thought I remembered. "But you had me convinced pretty quickly. I remember thinking these were really trippy. I'd like to read them *again*, actually."

"Oh," I said.

"I just never liked the way he drew knees."

You Don't Know Dick

1. Not like I do, anyway. Philip K. Dick (1928–1982) is the only prolific author whose whole life's work I can fairly claim to have read through *twice*, picayune exceptions notwithstanding—the fact that my eyes may have glazed over on a second pass at some of the lesser posthumous novels, or at the massive volumes of letters, is surely compensated by the fact that I've reread *Ubik*, *The Three Stigmata of Palmer Eldritch*, *Martian Time-Slip*, *A Scanner Darkly*, and a couple of other favorites three, four, even five times since my discovery of Dick, long ago, at age fifteen. He was my "favorite writer" ten years before the start of the publishing boom (Vintage Books is in the process of reissuing thirty-six of his books, good, bad, and lousy), and as formative an influence as marijuana or punk rock—as equally responsible for beautifully fucking up my life, for bending it irreversibly along a course I still travel. I find I need to spill this now, not (I hope) merely to establish provenance but to get on paper, before it is too late to recall, some glimpse of what the special condition known as "Dickheadedness" consisted of in the years after his death and before his current and ongoing canonization. As well, I need to warn you: Philip K. Dick's shelf is growing ever-more strange and misleading as it

makes contact with the outer reaches of his vast and woolly oeuvre. So I offer myself as a native guide.

2. The world doesn't need another introduction to or apologia for Philip K. Dick. There've been plenty. I've committed a few myself already. Between his hipster canonization, the frequency of academic and news-paper pundit citation, and the endless flow of Hollywood adaptations of his novels and stories, nobody much needs persuasion that Dick is *some* kind of important figure. Anyone who's taken the hint and cracked one of the books also knows he's many kinds of problematic—foremost in the disastrous unevenness of his prose, even within the space of a given page. He's that species of great writer, the uneven-prose species: Dickens, Dreiser, and Highsmith are others. Russians will tell you Dostoyevsky is too, and that we don't know this because translators have been covering his ass. Dick's ass, though, is uncoverable. His sentences routinely fall down and cry "ouch." In the words of Bob Dylan, another prolific and variable artist whose oeuvre offers pitfalls for newcomers, "I'm in love with the ugliest girl in the world!"

3. I'd read maybe a dozen of Dick's novels before I encountered the word *oeuvre*—maybe forty before I dared use it in a sentence. Dick vis-ited France ("I had the interesting experience of being famous") in 1974 and there possibly heard the word applied to his work. By that time his caustic and generous irony had mostly salved his raw sense of rejection by the literary establishment ("The only non-SF writer who ever treated me with courtesy was Herbert Gold, who I met at a literary party in San Francisco") and he might have enjoyed the use of the word, but likely wouldn't have identified much. I'd like to propose an alternative usage, *irv.* We'll speak of Dick's irv.

4. Uncertain of the value of their holdings, Vintage has chosen to pub-lish in bouquets. For instance, in May 2002, *Dr. Bloodmoney, Clans of the Alphane Moon, Time Out of Joint,* and *The Simulacra,* which is not a bad batch, not bad at all. In particular, *Dr. Bloodmoney* is one of Dick's most sympathetic and humane books of the early sixties (with *The Man in the*

High Castle and *Martian Time-Slip*), as well as one of the most capably (maybe I should say *least-badly*) written. *Time Out of Joint* is a dark-horse favorite, set in a Cheeveresque fifties suburb, and incorporating the flavor of Dick's realist novels (unpublished during his lifetime) into a pataphysical–*Twilight Zone* framework, only marred by a piss-poor ending. *Clans* is a cruel and antic psychiatric farce, written as if cribbed from the DSMR-IV; *Simulacra* a murkily overpopulated Balzacian social panorama. *Bloodmoney* and *Time* are crucial books. *Clans* and *Simulacra*, if not exactly ideal entry points into the irv, don't shame it.

5. Certainly none of this quartet risks turning off curious readers as do the previously republished *Game-Players of Titan*, *We Can Build You*, or the god-awful *World Jones Made*. Among the howlingly bad ones I'll single out *Vulcan's Hammer* for special shaming. When Dick potboiled the results were usually characteristically strange, but not so *Vulcan's Hammer*. Throw any fifteen out-of-print SF novels from 1954 into a blender—maybe you'd get *Vulcan's Hammer*, maybe something better.

6. When I was fifteen and sixteen I scoured Brooklyn's used bookstores and thrift shops for the hardest-to-find Dick titles, trying to complete a shelf of the thirty-seven-odd published works. This was 1979 and 1980, before Dick published his last three novels and died, and before the posthumous publication of a dozen or so manuscripts. Locating *Vulcan's Hammer* was a notable triumph. I'll always remember dowsing it out of a crate of moldering paperbacks that had been pushed beneath a shelf, dusting its glorious, hideous cover (Dick's biographer Lawrence Sutin describes it as occupying "deserved purgatory as half of a 1960 Ace Double") and more or less pinching myself in disbelief: *Vulcan's fucking Hammer!* I'd found it! Of course, then I had to go and read the damn thing. The irony is that out-of-printness served the purposes of exploring the irv nicely: the easiest books to find, and therefore the first I'd happened to read, were mostly Dick's masterpieces (*Castle*, *Ubik*, *Stigmata*, *Do Androids Dream of Electric Sheep?*). This was because the better books had received comparatively many reprintings, whereas the dreck was always the rarest essence. The problem nowadays is that Vintage's uniformly prestigious shelf of clean, authoritative editions disguises these natural hierarchies absolutely.

7. Would Dick have liked seeing *Vulcan's Hammer* rescued, and seated like a homunculus among the angels? Impossible to know. Late in life Dick saw odd virtues in his rottenest early works, partly because he tended to see all his previous novels and stories as precognitive glimpses of a religious revelation which overtook him in 1974—everything in his own history seemed to prefigure his conversion experience. Dick was a strange and difficult man, if famously enchanting to meet, and as his posthumous career expanded through the eighties—as the work became enshrined in academic and literary culture—it was hard not to speculate how completely the man's continued earthly existence might have screwed it up.

8. Of course, it's easy to oversimplify, and imagine that Dick's career splits cleanly into the disreputable past and the reputable present. In fact, the possibility that Dick was of dire and awesome literary significance haunts his reputation, such as it was, in the old SF ghetto. The back cover of the $1.50 1976 Ace Books reprint of *Simulacra* boasts: "The 21st Century. It was a shifting, shadowy and extraordinary world . . . and very dangerous . . ." But it also bears a blurb which reads: "If there is such a thing as 'black science fiction', Philip K. Dick is its Pirandello, its Becket and its Pinter . . ." That's Becket [*sic*].

9. The opposite applies: understanding of Dick's stature is still muddled by the appeal to mysticism his late work provides. Curious readers attracted by the advocacy of scholars and fellow writers may still be put off by an air of conspiracy theory, persecution ecstasy, and religious char-latanism in Dick's writing, or the woolly-eyed gullibility of some of his admirers. There surrounds Dick some stink of cultishness no number of Frederic Jameson citations can rub off.

10. If there ever was a cult, in 1984 I managed to sign up as its lieu-tenant. All through my high-school years I'd planned to visit California

and plant myself at the feet of my hero, but before I managed it, he died. So I clipped obituaries and went to college instead. When one of the clippings announced the formation of a Philip K. Dick Society, dedicated to propagating his works and furthering his posthumous career, my flame of pilgrimage was relit. I dropped out and hitchhiked west, and in Berkeley I looked up Paul Williams—not the short blond songwriter, but the *Crawdaddy*-founding rock critic who'd written about Dick for *Rolling Stone* and become the estate's literary executor—he was wearing a Meat Puppets T-shirt the day I found him. Paul made immediate good use of me, mostly for licking stamps. I hosted the PKD Society's envelope-stuffing parties in my Berkeley apartment, two blocks from the tiny, wood-frame house where Dick had lived during the writing of his first ten or so novels. And, a great thrill, I later sold the Dick estate a few dozen of the hundreds of spare copies of paperbacks I'd assembled—my book hunting had become obsessive, and I by then owned three, four, and even five copies of most of the dozens of out-of-print titles. The estate didn't. In order to "further his posthumous career," Paul needed copies of the rarest books to send to prospective publishers like Vintage. *Vulcan's Hammer*, in other words, is sort of my fault.

11. In my role as Paul's sidekick, I got a chance to sort through acres of letters, outlines for novels never written, and personal ephemera, like Dick's lease for an apartment in Fullerton ("two neutered cats okay"), which for some reason I photocopied and have kept to this day. I once handled Dick's personal copy of the *I Ching* (any reader of *The Man in the High Castle* knows the talismanic importance of that text), its hard covers softened and swollen from use, like Ahab's Bible retrieved from the Pequod. The book was full of paper slips in Dick's handwriting, desperate inquiries into everyday subjects on which Dick had turned to the oracle for consultation: *Will (editor X) accept the new draft of Policeman? Should I lend Y money for Seconal? Will Z sleep with me?* I also once owned a single gold earring made by Dick's jeweler wife, another *Man in the High Castle*-related fetish. The earring was stolen by an ex-girlfriend who didn't understand its importance—who found my obsession with Dick embarrassing.

12. When Vintage completes the cycle, it will have made available all of the fifties and sixties SF novels—the ten or fifteen excellent books which originally made Dick's underground reputation and the twenty-some weaker titles which always kept that reputation hobbled. In the mid-eighties, before the Vintage reissues, the only one of those books which was at all easy to find was the Del Rey Books *Blade Runner* tied-in reprint of *Do Androids Dream of Electric Sheep?* But for the collectors and cognoscenti (all six hundred of us) who were tuned into Paul's PKD Society newsletters, the market was flooded with outré material just reaching first light in expensive small-press hardcovers—*Ubik: The Screenplay*, *The Dark-Haired Girl* (essays), *Nick and the Glimmung* (a children's book), five volumes of *Selected Letters*, and enough unpublished realist novels from his thwarted "mainstream" efforts of the fifties to make up another writer's whole career: *Mary and the Giant*, *The Broken Bubble*, *Gather Yourselves Together*, *In Milton Lumky Territory*, *The Man Whose Teeth Were All Exactly Alike*, *Humpty Dumpty in Oakland*, and *Puttering About in a Small Land*. These were works never published during Dick's lifetime, all made easily available—for a brief moment, anyway. Now the situation is exactly reversed: those titles have all slipped back into the mists, and that list I've just typed out might serve to fuel another fifteen-year-old's obsessive quest. In a sense, the "lost" and the "found" Dick have swapped places, twice.

13. It's hard to make a case for the realist novels. The implicit assertion of the Dick credibility-boom goes something like this: *There's this writer who works with the pop-culture iconography of science fiction but with such mad originality and verve—and emotional intensity—that he created his own personal genre, surrealistic and freewheeling, with enormous capacities for humor, despair, and for making a sophisticated critique of capitalist culture (despite, ahem, infelicities in the prose). He deserves your serious attention as much as any realist writer.* This was a bunch to swallow in the first place. It's asking a huge latitude of the guardians of our literary culture to then say: *Oh yeah, that same guy, the visionary pop-culture surrealist? Well, he also wrote these eight puzzling and unforgettable novels in a dour, lower-middle-class realist mode—something like Richard Yates meets*

Charles Willeford. These too, deserve a look (despite, ahem, infelicities in the prose). That double reverse may simply be too much.

14. Nevertheless, even the very worst of those realist novels would better reward your time than *Vulcan's Hammer*. Not to be a bully.

15. I can't keep from comparisons to other artists whose sprawling fecundity makes any such essay as this the equivalent of providing the reader an umbrella before ushering him out the door into a hurricane. So—just to focus again for a moment, on that bouquet of titles I mentioned before—if Dick is Hitchcock, then *Dr. Bloodmoney* is his *The Trouble with Harry* (perverse pastoral). If he's Altman, *Simulacra* is *A Wedding* (underrated but overcomplicated), and *The Clans of the Alphane Moon* is *Beyond Therapy* (disturbed). If he's Graham Greene, *Time Out of Joint* is *Brighton Rock*, but if he's Dylan it's *Another Side*. If he's Picasso—oh, never mind.

16. In a review of Joseph McBride's eight-hundred-page master biography of John Ford, Jonathan Rosenbaum notes that in the galley copy McBride had sliced through the thicket to provide a "Ford's Top Ten Films"—but then cut it out of the final book. I wonder, was McBride afraid of being too final? Or was he embarrassed that, for all his scholarship, he had a fondness for "top-ten lists"? Let me not deny this service—after all, I've only been adjusting and polishing this list in my head for the majority of my life. So, the irv de la irv, in no particular order: *Castle, Stigmata, Ubik, Valis, Androids, Bloodmoney, The Transmigration of Timothy Archer, A Scanner Darkly, Martian Time-Slip, Confessions of a Crap Artist*—wait, shit, okay, fifteen—*Now Wait for Last Year, Time Out of Joint, A Maze of Death, Galactic Pot-Healer* . . .

17. Perhaps I fear that if I ever finish this list—the making of which is an extension of my obsessive searching in bookstores for Dick's books, even after I'd found them all—I will die. Or grow up. Similarly, this is probably the right place to admit that I've never actually read *Gather Yourselves Together*. I suppose the truth is that I'm saving it.

Lives of the Bohemians

I learned to think by watching my father paint. I wrote that sentence five years ago, in a brief essay for the catalogue of a ten-year retrospective exhibition of my father's paintings by a small museum in New England. More recently I've helped him archive a cache of his canvases from the 1970s, many of which I'd not seen since he painted them—that is to say, since childhood. Confronting an array of pictures spanning my own life on this planet, I was struck again with their implicit challenge to my understanding. Could I think about the paintings themselves? Tell Richard Lethem something about them he didn't know? I'd begun to see my father's work (and his life) as being defined by a resistance to—and reluctance to assume—conventional authority. To write about him while he still lived, I'd need to borrow some of his disobedience. I wanted to try.

Yet I find myself in relation to father and paintings as the apes in *2001: A Space Odyssey* stood before their monolith. Dumb, though making noise. Weren't those apes supposed to grab an implement and get to work? After all, it was me that put *think* and *my father paint* in the same sentence.

As a teenager I revered Stanley Kubrick, and Arthur C. Clarke—at some point I'd have called them my favorite director and favorite writer (though Clarke was shed years sooner than Kubrick). And probably, as choices of favorites, Kubrick and Clarke formed an armor against threatening aspects of my father's art, and of my parents' world, and of our family's life. They offered images the surfaces of which were clean of the paint-drippy, hippie-drippy, Bob Dylan–raspy-voiced, imperfection-embracing chaos surrounding me everywhere. And as images of the artist, Kubrick and Clarke felt somehow absolute in their stances of confidence, of magisterial indifference. (I know better now, but it doesn't seem mistaken that each of these artists particularly *wished* to make that impression—enough to fool a kid.) So they made an antidote for the drug of proximity to my dad—an artist whose authority was for me both bigger and smaller, more problematic in every way.

Like that ape, gazing at his monolith, my attempt here is in the nature of a scientific inquiry under impossible conditions. I set out to write about a painter. He happens to be my father. Who was married to my mother. Who—parents, together with my brother and sister—make up my family. All I know comes from the ground I gaze across, and am rooted to, helplessly. What's to keep the paintings from slipping out of view below the horizon, as my planet of memory grumbles on its axis?

As late as 1966, at the age of thirty-four, my father's trajectory was a fine and ordinary one, for a serious painter of his generation. I mean, rather than for a person of his small-town Midwestern upbringing, which might not have indicated that a serious young man would look to become a serious painter of his generation. The last of six siblings raised in Missouri and Iowa, Richard Lethem's childhood straddled the Depression and the Second World War, the war in which two of his older brothers, and his sisters' husbands, fought—men vacating the scene while a boy stayed behind with sisters and sisters-in-law, who might have seemed more like a batch of adoring young aunts.

My father's own European tour was on a Fulbright to Paris, in 1959, where he studied at the Grand Chaumière. That, following a bachelor's degree begun at the Kansas City Art Institute and completed at Columbia, and a master's, also at Columbia. I own a student painting from that time, not an "original" Lethem but rather a tricky quotation canvas, done to accompany his undergraduate thesis on De Chirico. In it my father, painting in De Chirico's style, has replaced the Italian's vacated piazzas and marble busts with Midwestern American iconography: a warehouse, some farm machinery, a kernel of candy corn. And a bare blue lightbulb dangles from a socket, harkening forward to Guston.

My father would soon make much both of this surrealist-pictorial impulse, pointing from De Chirico to Guston, and of his eagerness to paint farm machinery and other tools. But, as a young painter at the end of the fifties, he first had to add his hurried contribution to the waning stream of abstract expressionism. De Kooning was his prime hero. Kline and Gorky not far behind. The first ambitious paintings (meaning, in that era, the first *large* paintings) of his life were warm, dappled abstractions, painted with a dripping brush, evocative of landscapes. They were good. They were shown. They made no huge dent in the world, as new abstract paintings mostly didn't in 1960, and before I was born he was done making them.

My maternal grandfather, whom I would never meet, fled his wife and New York when my mother was three, to repatriate in East Germany. The improbable gesture likely speaks to how much more German than Jewish he felt—and how Communist, as well. My grandmother was another secular Jew and defiant leftist, but also a born New Yorker, irascible as Thelma Ritter, buddy to cops and cabdrivers, lover of pizza and egg creams. She worked as an accountant in a pickle factory in Sunnyside, Queens, and raised her single child to share her secular passion for Abraham Lincoln, for books, arguments, and causes.

My mother dropped out of Queens College in 1962, drawn to Greenwich Village thrills. There she pierced ears, with a pin and ice cube, at a jewelry shop on MacDougal Street, and palled around with folksingers: Tuli Kupferberg, Dave Van Ronk, Phil Ochs. In 1963 she met my father, the bearded painter. By the time I was born, in early 1964, they lived in an illegal loft on West Broadway. In that loft, in that year, high on love, sex, and procreation, and on the cultural possibilities in the air (in my firm opinion), high on William Blake (by his own testimony), and likely sometimes high on pot (my mother, like John Lennon, loved to turn you on), Richard Lethem changed his painting style entirely.

In what became, from 1963 to 1968, a first major phase in his art, my father started painting *stuff*. The De Chirico influence realized now, the pictures featured functional objects charged with a mysterious significance, and raised to the level of the iconographic: basketball hoops, vises, stereopticons, and salesman's or traveler's trunks. My father also painted a series of struck matches, beheld from one side, their sizzled black heads surrounded by a penumbra of sensationally colorful flame. The presentation in the paintings of this period, though hard-edged, never bore even a trace of pop chill; his brushwork held to expressionist drama, his palette to earthly, or fleshly, warmth.

That work, beginning the year of my birth, became an explosion of canvases in 1966 and 1967, in his studio in Kansas City, Missouri. There, my father had taken a teaching job at the Art Institute. He'd converted the barefoot Jewish folksinger girl into a campus wife, was on track for tenure, and was jubilantly painting in an individual and highly recognizable style—as I said, my father's trajectory was, at one point, just about perfect for a serious painter of his moment, and for a serious bohemian. A dashing professor with a beard and, as yet, no dangerous affiliations.

Five years ago I wrote: "In my father's earlier 'symbolist/surrealist' phase, the work, though physical in its voracious painterliness, speaks of the human presence mostly by implication and absence. The empty trunks and lonely vises and stereopticons of this period have a Magritte-like conceptual/literary authority, but their owners and makers have flown the coop." My father himself has written: "I see those images of trunks, vises, and basketball hoops as enchanted erotic objects which came from a period of great personal fulfillment and love."

What I want to admit now is that as a child I always preferred the paintings from 1964 to 1967 to the work I witnessed my father making in Brooklyn, in the 1970s. I fetishized the clarity of that depopulated world of fetish objects. The paintings seemed clean to me. I likely associated them with the emotional reality of an infant who has his parents all to himself; in Kansas City we lived in a vast stone house on campus, surrounded by a sculpture garden. It made a citadel for the triad of mother, father, and child. It was the perfect opposite of a neighborhood.

The "Fort Hood Three" were U.S. Army privates who declined to be returned to Vietnam. The war, they explained, never officially declared, was "illegal and immoral." Court-martialed in July of 1966, their lawyers tried to call Robert McNamara to the stand. The judge made it simple: "This is a case against the United States, and the United States has not consented to be sued." The soldiers got three-to-five. When the Three were shifted to the federal prison at Leavenworth, Kansas, in January of 1967, a small group of peace marchers showed up too. These ninety-odd peaceniks were greeted with snowballs and jeers from other citizens, who'd come to rain contempt on the dissident soldiers. The marchers sang "We Shall Overcome." A blare of Sousa, played from a truck, drowned them out.

My parents were among those ninety, even partly responsible for the march. My father, who stood at the microphone at the scuttled rally, had become faculty adviser for a chapter of Students for a Democratic Society, while my mother had begun draft counseling ("It's better to run to Toronto") draft-eligible art students. That same spring, my father organized an all-day Saturday teach-in on campus. That Saturday the institute's president, inflamed by phone calls from trustees concerned about his grip on the faculty, arrived in person and got into a comical shoving match with my father, in a stairwell.

C'est la tenure. My parents, though, had already decided to throw over Kansas City, and my father to throw over teaching. As Dylan would say, "I'm going back to New York City, I do believe I've had enough." For my mother, who didn't drive a car (cast-iron New Yorker, she never learned), the Midwest isolation was suffocating. And my father? He explained later, "I wanted to reject the Establishment institutions that were going along with the war. And I found the strident voices of opposition in my head were making it hard to listen to students."

I retain discontinuous memories of Kansas City: I recall the sculpture garden, for instance, but no protest marches. I remember petting a dog, and riding on my grandfather's tractor, but no hippies. The hippies I got to know later. Yet I've rehearsed my father's break with his teaching at Kansas City because it seems a key to my father's painting (or, sometimes, lack of painting) in the fifteen years that followed.

The key to more than that, really. In my parents' "rejection" of "Establishment institutions" I sense the parameters within which my personality grew; the parameters that, like those of any childhood (apart from the most exalted or depraved), I both bloomed within, like the windows of a greenhouse, and rattled against, like the jaws of a trap. The place our family delivered itself to—a debilitated but gorgeous row house in a Brooklyn neighborhood called Gowanus, or Boerum Hill—was to be the stage for it all: painting, family, childhood.

Once in Brooklyn my parents' lives were not just overtly political. They became countercultural, as opposed to merely hip. Baby Jonathan's eerie little modernist world was soon filling up with siblings, neighbors, commune-housemates (for our home became a commune, of sorts), and the terrifying richness of a neighborhood full of race and class juxtapositions. My parents also opened their marriage, and my world had to make room for the inkling, later the certainty, that some of their friends were lovers. My father's canvases, when he resumed painting in the early seventies, were loaded with human figures, many unclothed, all of them embodying in different ways the forms of human chaos, the daily politics, that our lives had become.

I don't think I was autistic, but like an autistic child I wanted the human volume turned down. Though consciously thrilled by the adult lives around me, and the odd but definite privileges my communion with their variety had bestowed, I was unconsciously seeking hiding places. I developed a craving, not only in my father's work but generally, for remote, depopulated art, for images of sublime alienation. I held out hope of cultivating a discrete and unaffiliated, even solipsistic persona. No wonder I wanted De Chirico back, or pined for Stanley Kubrick. My own early writing was the pure product of this taste, emulating Clarke, Kafka, Philip K. Dick, Graham Greene, Stanislaw Lem, and Borges.

We lived in the house while my father renovated it by hand, teaching himself the carpentry skills, the laborer's trade, that would become his livelihood for the next twenty years. Our home was soon a stopping-off point for former colleagues and students of my father's who'd arrived in New York and needed a place to stay, as well as for old friends from Greenwich Village, recontacted after the Kansas City interlude. My mother's instincts as a host and raconteur made our kitchen table a site of meetings, transformations, flirtations, arguments.

We found comrades in the neighborhood. Alongside shabby rooming houses, alongside black and Puerto Rican families entrenched in a neighborhood that had been mostly abandoned by New York's white-immigrant middle classes many decades earlier, and alongside the new white renovators who'd launched an unsystematic gentrification a stone's throw from a jail and two housing projects, Boerum Hill was home to communes. At least five or six of the cheaply rented row houses within the immediate blocks had been colonized by groups of radicals, singles, and couples just out of college, and making their home in an affordable quarter. These houses had flavors: one might be firmly Marxist, another druggy, another more familial, given an anchor, say, by a divorced mom raising a kid or two.

Ours was a quasi-commune, one with a family at its center and a painter's studio on the top floor. My parents extended their commitment to causes along every open path: my father taught home repair to teenagers at a settlement house, and art workshops to prisoners in the Brooklyn House of Detention. They both went on protesting the war until the war ran out, and marched in favor of day care centers, and against proposed Robert Moses freeways and nuclear power. Each time my mother went to the supermarket she shifted heads of iceberg lettuce and bunches of grapes picked by exploited migrant workers into the ice-cream section of the supermarket, to be destroyed by freezing. She had that streak of yippie in her, and was also once ticketed by a transit cop for using a slug in place of a subway token—her protest, I suppose, against fare increases.

The neighborhood was a laboratory, a zone of mixing, never defined by one ethnicity or class. Mongrel by deep nature, the place absorbed the first scattering of hippies, homosexuals, and painters pretty ungrudgingly. But with signs of a real-estate boom, and a broad displacement of the existing population, the changes were politicized. Our family was drawn into the discomfiting issue of gentrification. We were against it, ideologically. Yet my mother's native-outerborough gregariousness was a force in the making of a new community; by helping knit the white families to the existing neighborhood, she encouraged pioneers, I think. And my father's trade was a paradox. Having fled ivory tower for blue-collar solidarity, he soon became a highly sought renovation specialist, a cabinetmaker and sash-and-jamb restorer with an artist's touch. So he was engaged on a daily basis in rehabbing the brownstones of Boerum Hill for their new owners, gentrifying with his hands.

Sure, we felt the risk of involuntary complicity. We were white families in a minority neighborhood, no way out of that. Symbolic alliances were therefore everything, and neighbors could become rather paranoid. Those who shared our devotions monitored others for insensitivities or worse. New homeowners galvanizing themselves against a rash of burglaries, or urging the sprucing up of a vacant lot, might be guilty of collusion with Establishment institutions, and those, we knew, led straight to Nixon, and the war.

I don't mean to be flippant. Boerum Hill, like any zone "revived" by white homeownership, was prey to cynical speculation. And, as many an enemies list or secret memo has shown, the paranoids were right. The idealisms of that hour actually now impress me as a gossamer lost world, Proustian in its delicacy. Those shades in the spectrum between *radical* and *guilty liberal*, parsed with such intensity at the time, strike me as poignant from this vantage. Even the uptightest adults I knew as a child nonetheless regarded Watergate and Vietnam as proof our leaders were corrupt, and probably sexually hung up as well. And my parents' reluctance to be seen as gentrifiers was largely an instinctive pleasure in the neighborhood as they found it.

My father's art also became communized. His studio was opened to family and friends and to other artists, as well as to a stream of nude models. For a few years he merely drew, dodging, for a time, the ambition and expense of oil on canvas. Or were canvas and oil also suspect, for a time, of being in collusion with Establishment institutions? Instead he drew portraits and nudes, in oil crayon and pencil and sometimes with a wash of brushwork, on sheets of vinyl. The portraits collected our friends and neighbors, of all colors, frequently with their lips parted in mid-conversation. The nudes, of both sexes, were delicate, and sometimes explicit.

At the center of my father's art practice, at the start of the seventies, was "drawing group." This was a weekly gathering—sometimes in his studio, but most regularly in the Brooklyn loft of a couple of friends, Bob and Cynthia—of artists who wished to work from a model in the nude. Taking turns arranging for a model, they'd then each chip in the five or six bucks it took to pay the fee. On nights when a model didn't show up, a few members of the group might take turns shedding clothes to serve in their place. These artists, a shifting cast of seven or eight regulars, were younger than my dad, and none as trained. Yet there was no question that they gathered as other than peers. The drawing group wasn't set apart from the life of our neighborhood, but rather included people I knew from communes, from my mother's table. Cynthia ran a local children's bookstore. Bob was one of my father's carpentry partners. The group also included one of my family's own housemates, Nancy. And, for a while, me.

When my father began painting again in the seventies he made the drawing group his subject. The new canvases featured nude models, often, but not always, female. Many also presented some figure of a painter, or watcher, always male. In one sense, this "artists-and-models" subject was highly traditional. (My father, in a dismissive moment, called these paintings "European.") The work nudged Courbet, Manet, Picasso, calling up an old self-validating drama of the male spectator, recessed in the shadows or glimpsed at one side, in the self-portraitist's mirror. Here was the painter as an implicit figure of authority, a step apart from life, and for the viewer a flattering surrogate: Apollonian, noncommittal, masterful.

Yet these pictures also undermined or teased that authority. Just as he'd thrown over teaching, and now worked in the company of those who could have been his students, by making the group his subject my father abjured the privilege of an artist's exclusive sensibility. *Drawing Group #1* is an example: while the male artist considers a model stretched prone, limbs flung for a gaze-banquet, in the foreground a female artist refines a sketch from an earlier pose. On her pad the nude sits, elbow on knee, an asexual crouch. The disagreement gently mocks erotic wish fulfillment: the pose we're shown in the painting is just one among many, hardly inevitable. The painter making use of the model hasn't disregarded the group who'll chip in to cover the cost (each, we hope, having gotten at least five bucks' worth of poses they liked too).

Or take *Turning*, finished in 1979. This scene, which began as a simple life study, evolved into a self-conscious drama of mortality, inspired by Rilke's *Sonnets to Orpheus*. A heroic and vulnerable male nude glances backward at Death the Watcher, who takes the form of an artist standing dispassionately at a drawing table, in deep shadows. But leavening the scene is, again, a series of confessions of a painter's studio shared with other bodies, with other agendas. A sketcher's pad intrudes from the lower right. A hand pokes in, to pat the head of a wolfish dog. The model's robe hangs on a peg, alongside a claw hammer. Robe and hammer forecast the future of the players in this allegory: one will don the robe (it's chilly in this studio), then his street clothes. The other, resume his labors as a carpenter. There are kids to feed. The dog too.

Variations in degrees of "realism" confound these paintings. So do weird conflations of planar space—shades, again, of De Chirico. In my father's own thinking, recaptured for me in a recent letter, he'd framed a couple of questions: "How to capture the psychic energy and urgency implied in realism without the dead end of imitation. Not being satisfied to reduce things to generalities—instead wanting the unpurified, tangible quality of experience to come through." And: "How to eliminate the narrow confines of modernist style without falling into sentimentality."

My father had seemingly disabled the symbolic and conceptual levels in his painting (all the stuff I pined for, as a child, in preferring the sixties work). In truth, though, his "realist" paintings were full of gestures of grotesquerie and invention. Imagined figures crept onto the canvases, and cartoonish expressions of lust, impatience, or childlike reverie crept over the faces of the artists and models. At the same time, backdrops are strewn with the prosaic: books, workmen's boots or gloves, coffee mugs, playing cards, documentary touches to decant any psychosexual theatrics. And that shaggy gray dog, mooning at the feet of the models. The dog's name is Blue. He must have been lonely when we kids were off at school.

As a puppy, Blue was rescued from the street. My mother found him in a state of cringing fear, and near starvation. The dog's condition wasn't a mystery, though. He'd been kept in the side yard of the home of a Puerto Rican family two houses away, and my parents had seen him cowering under the hand of their teenage boys' merry violence for weeks before he'd been set loose on the street.

"The Green House Kids," as my family called the teeming inhabitants of that ramshackle structure, were a foul bunch. Not that we allowed ourselves to say so at the time. Instead, I and my siblings fostered what now strikes me as a hysterical myth of displacement: we credited our discomfort to the dog, who, we were positive we could determine, "didn't like Puerto Ricans," and of course couldn't be blamed. We got to marvel at his prejudice, guilt free. The parable of Blue's grudge was a container for our reluctance to give a certain thing its name: we liked plenty of Puerto Ricans, but the nearest at hand, the Green House Kids, were pretty awful.

Blue bore this responsibility nobly, as he did everything. He was a beautiful member of the family.

Open marriage turned to separation in 1975. My father moved out of the house for a while, at one point into another Brooklyn commune, a neighborhood away. I'd say this was the worst thing that could have happened, except that denial has obliterated all but the curiosity I felt, to a point of exhilaration, at the expansion of my world to this new turf. Just for instance, one of the guys in the new commune was just out of NYU film school, and deep into *Star Trek*, my favorite television show after *The Twilight Zone*. He put my brother and me into his movie, which was being shot on three adjacent rooftops of differing heights, to symbolize the class system in America. My brother and I played the middle-class kids. We got to fling garbage off our roof, onto the heads of the poor.

Anyway, the worst thing that could have happened happened next. My mother fell ill, suffering seizures first taken for epilepsy, but soon diagnosed as symptoms of a brain tumor. This drew our family into one place again, and my father's studio back into our upper floor. My father's intensity of purpose didn't waver; in fact, the body of late-seventies work really begins after my mother's diagnosis. This was with her passionate encouragement. She sat for him constantly, in her robe, and out of it. The portraits from that year record the patchwork progress of her hair's regrowth, after being shaved for incisions on her skull, and after her follicles' damage by radiation.

With the drawing group, and his wife, in this era my father also painted his kids (always fully clothed, though it was a reasonably nudist household). I recall sitting for a portrait with my hands folded, wearing an orange Mets wristband. Though I usually killed posing time by reading in his studio, my father didn't want a book in this painting. He wanted to see my eyes. In the painting that resulted I sit in the crossroads, bracketed by my father's palette table and a mirror in which he could see himself; both table and father appear in the portrait.

My father had opened the doors of his studio to the ordinary days of his house. While chasing a "European" theme, his voracious brush gobbled life into the frame. The subject, literal and sublimated, is family, community, and the counterculture, that circle of sympathetic souls into which he'd dissolved his pipe-and-elbow-patches authority. The questing, pensive, contradictory attitudes of the models and the artists, the friends and family and imagined figures arrayed in these pictures tell of the nourishing warmth but also the tenuousness, and sometimes the sexual disarray, of a life lived in the embrace of communal ideals.

In one of the most free and instinctive paintings from this period, *Loft*, the cast is reduced to painter and model (not to mention the dog).

She reads, while he greets the viewer head-on, fingers full of brushes, and stripped of reserve in the simplest way—he's naked too. The title, and the youthfulness of the bemused, tousled painter, link it to a halcyon year of discovery: 1963–64, to Richard and Judith alone in the loft on West Broadway. It's no self-portrait. The woman doesn't resemble my mother, or the painter my father. But the rhapsodic brushwork emphasizes the unguarded intimacy of the scene, a page torn from a dream diary in the lives of the bohemians.

Judith Lethem died of cancer at the age of thirty-six. Her death was, of course, a private passage, yet the long illness which she and we endured seemed inextricable from the battles of our family's life in those years. The souring of utopian optimism in the mid-seventies, a historical cliché, was for us true, and personal. Even before her illness, my family's difference ensured we could feel superior and magical, or freakish and tragic, but never ordinary. What set us apart as artists or potential artists, and as hippies, protesters, commune dwellers, Quakers, white kids but in public school, all seemed to foretell our special fate, an uncanny story destined, not justly but perhaps somehow appropriately, for an end in hospitals and jails, or an early funeral.

How personal? My mother was one of the "Capitol Steps Thirteen," a group wrongly arrested during a Washington, D.C., protest for occupying what the ACLU would later prove, in a lawsuit on their behalf, to be public space. She was pregnant with my sister, Mara, at the time. We three kids bragged of this legacy, relishing details such as the slices of baloney the arrestees liberated from their jailhouse sandwiches and slapped up against the wall in protest of their treatment. But we also must have been haunted by the tale, by images of our mom and dad as inhabitants of a sphere of jubilant stridency (electrified by bolts of persecution mania) so beyond the usual boundaries of a family's life.

If my mother was remarkable then it had to cut both ways. The horrendous diagnosis could only be more evidence of how remarkable she was, signal, not noise, in our interpretation of our family's place in the world. If our sense of special artistic and political purpose was to be preserved, it would have to conform to tragic destiny as my mother fell ill, just as it would need to encompass the world's resistance to our standards, made official a few years later by the ascendance of Reagan. The conflation was made, briefly, explicit: we, or at least I, succumbed to the temptation to blame my mother's brain tumor on Ulano, the toxin-belching solvent factory two blocks away on Bergen Street, and tangible like a punch to the nose for many more blocks around. Here was a chance to widen the circle of chaos and catastrophe from the family, outward to the environment, the political moment.

Ulano, a squat, windowless monstrosity situated exactly between the Wyckoff Gardens housing projects and the gentrifying street I grew up on, had been listed in an EPA report as one of the nation's ten worst urban polluters. After my mother's death my father spearheaded the neighborhood's organized resistance to its undiluted foulness, really the last of his and therefore my family's sequence of great causes. In truth, if my mother's brain cancer had an external cause it was likely a bad batch of polio vaccine, whose nightmarish delayed effects on its recipients, neatly matching my mother's case, were only traced three decades later. The faulty vaccine was distributed in Queens and Brooklyn in the mid-fifties, the span when my mother would have been immunized.

As a parent, Judith was a passionate advocate, never abdicating an inch of her ferocious scrutiny of our lives until illness made that scrutiny impossible. But what she advocated was paradoxical: freedom, and responsibility for the results of our own choices. She debunked custodial authority, as my father debunked painterly authority. An example: my first chance to smoke pot came in her presence, when I was eleven. I'd been sitting with a group of her late-night friends around our kitchen table when a joint was produced and lit. One of the guests, a newcomer, a man (I mean, he was probably twenty-one or twenty-two; he wouldn't impress me as a man *now*) seemed surprised she didn't object to my presence—titillated too. Raising the stakes to provoke her response, he passed the joint to me.

"He'll make his own decision," my mother announced, with pride. It was a declaration that dictated its own truth. She bet right; I passed the joint along, unpuffed. I saved my own first drug experiences for late nights with my peers, instead of hers, a couple of years later. Fate then robbed me of my chance to smoke my mother's drug of choice, and my own, with Judith. But I grasped my options. And my stance toward drugs, inscribed in that moment, was her testament: no right and wrong outside the user's (or refuser's) personal sense of rightness or wrongness. The only certain wrong at my mother's table was the hippie's hypocritical gesture, his drug prurience. And, with my help, she'd put him in his place.

I joined the drawing group in the year before my mother's death, and attended sporadically for a year or so after. In this same period I applied to Music and Art High School, got in, and went. I'd drawn and painted since before I could remember (and I would carry on for a while after my focus had shifted to narrative, to film, comics, and fiction). But at thirteen I wanted to be my dad in the most literal way.

I was also a fake, being thirteen. At the Thursday night meetings of the group I drew but also soaked in the scene. Ever eager for talk to resume, I hated the long poses, rooting most of all for that moment when someone would go around the corner to the German delicatessen for beer, soda, and imported chocolate cookies. I felt watchful, but I'd be flattering myself to claim I was a fly on the wall. The truth is I strolled around between poses as everyone did, making quasi-astute comments on the grown-ups' sketches.

You'd think I was taken with the bodies. I kept a partition, though, between my typically churning curiosity and this sober feast of blatant nudity all laid out before me. I was sure the kind of women's bodies I ravished in my mind's eye had nothing in common with the models' bodies to which I had regular viewing access, dumb as that sounds. In fact, I entertained crushes on a couple of the women in the drawing group, who never stepped out of their clothes. They were alive to my imagination. The naked ladies shed a light that blinded.

Encouraging me, my father also inadvertently funded a grotesquely exuberant ego. When I was fifteen, my mother dead for less than a year, I said something that upset him. My father and I were walking together, down Nevins Street, in daylight. I was bragging, I think, about the quality of my figure drawing, when I suggested that I was ready for a show. An exhibition of my drawings.

I got as far as asking whether his own gallery would be interested. The work I had in mind was done in the drawing group, a series of brightly colored pastels on thick white boards, which were in fact the discarded centers of picture mats, salvaged from some framer's shop, in the jackdaw manner of both my father's studio and his carpentry workshop.

He stopped us on the sidewalk. "Are you serious?" he asked.

"Sure."

"Do you really think you're ready, Jonathan?"

I'd located that rarity, my father's open temper. It was as though I'd probed for the limit of his antiauthoritarian ethos, and found it: an ape may grope a monolith, or a cat look at a king, but a child was not yet an artist. I think all of Richard Lethem's training, his degrees, his Fulbright, the pride of his guild, reared in him at that moment. The look on his face then seemed to encompass a disbelief in all that living had cost this artist, since the journey from West Broadway and Kansas City to Brooklyn, and from professordom to carpentry. Most of all in the unfathomable loss of his wife, that champion of his painter's prerogatives, his painter's days— and the mother of this damnable stripling.

The first question I remember asking about my father's painting is: "Why are the drips there?" I asked it of my mother. I knew it wasn't impossible to neaten up the drips; I'd seen my father's care in stretching a canvas, stippling a perfect pen-and-ink daffodil for an announcement of my sister's birth, or grouting tile work.

My mother's explanation was partly tautological. She told me that in paintings, drips were good. They gave evidence of the painter's hand at work—well, they sure do, I thought. Rather than offer words like *immediacy* or *expressionist* to an eight-year-old, she tried an analogy: the paint drips were like the squeak of acoustic guitar strings audible in recordings of the folksingers we loved to play in that house—Phil Ochs, Burl Ives, Pete Seeger. Once she pointed them out I wasn't sure I liked the guitar squeaks either. But her comparison has never been completely out of my mind since.

Seven or eight years later I was an adherent of what seemed to me dripless, squeakless art. The aforementioned icons of alienation—Kubrick, Borges, and Rod Serling. I was into punk, but not messy punk: I liked the Ramones, and Devo, and Talking Heads; above all I identified with David Byrne's grooming. When no one was looking I sold my mother's old Jimi Hendrix and Delaney and Bonnie LPs, which no one was playing now anyway. For my father's birthday I gave him a monograph on Magritte, a painter I knew he regarded as slick and illustrational. The gift was a heavy-handed suggestion that he ought to reconsider everything, come over to the glossily paranoid and solipsistic side of life before it was too late, as though only I knew where the action was.

I was utterly the product of his and my mother's sensibility, of course, but I desperately needed to convert it into something unrecognizable as such, to my father and myself. So I poured my graphic talents into hand-drawn comic books, my neophyte writing into science fiction, aspirations calculated to fly under the radar of my father's generationally typical notion of what could and couldn't be regarded as art.

Discomfort with my parents' politics I converted too, into a blithe and arrogant certainty that some advance in human evolution was the only hope for the species. This was a blend of Kubrick's mordant certainty as to the human need for self-destruction and the optimist view of Arthur C. Clarke (and of the whole space-goofy wing of the science-fiction genre), that humanity would outgrow its wretched cradle—the same mixture that lent *2001: A Space Odyssey* such an enthralling ambivalence.

Sometime in the eighties, when my father's outrage was focused on Guatemala or Nicaragua, he gleaned my indifference to the latest cause. I explained by loftily quoting Arthur C. Clarke (who was, I think, quoting, or paraphrasing, the British scientist J.B.S. Haldane): "Man must not export his borders into space." We're talking about the period in my life known as "high school," so this was loosely translatable as *Fuck you, Dad!* But I hadn't used those exact words, so we managed to eke out the following exchange, my father's incredulity mushrooming as it had when I requested an exhibition at his gallery.

Son: "That's why the search for extraterrestrial intelligence is so important, Dad. When we meet an alien race we'll understand that we're all one planet, and wars will be looked on as primitive behavior."

Father: "Are you saying that a world government is likely anytime soon? Or would be a *good* thing?"

Son: "If not in your lifetime, certainly in mine."

That's all I can bear to remember. Anyway, the point about space, I see now, was this: in space, no one can hear the guitar squeak. Or see the paint drip.

Evenings in our communal household, in the years after Judith's death, we cooked and washed dishes according to a weekly schedule. One of my dish nights, after a dinner where I'd not spoken a word, radiating sullen-teenage death rays instead, my father dried dishes in exchange for a moment alone with me. Piercing my cone of silence at the sink, he asked what was wrong. I played dumb—my behavior seemed normal enough to me. He pointed to my silence at dinner.

I offered another patronizing, Kubrickian explanation: "You have to understand, Dad, I'm a misanthrope."

I probably thought the word meant *someone who doesn't live in a commune.*

I'd never stopped looking at his paintings. I looked at them in sessions with him in the studio, dispensing approval and criticism with a teen's certainty. And I looked at them by myself, afternoons when he was out of the house. I often skulked in his studio, not only because, as I grew older, less interested in adults than in my own adultesque drama, the telephone there was the most private for marathon phone mopes with out-of-town girlfriends.

One day I committed a ridiculously Oedipal crime: I "fixed" a line in one of his paintings, while it hung in a near-finished state on his studio wall. It was a picture that engaged and, I guess, irritated me. The line at a woman's calf was interrupted—cruddy, it seemed to me, where it could be lucid. More cartoonish and perfect. So, drunk on my own gall, I swirled a brush in moist paint and clarified the line. The adjustment was negligible. That didn't keep me from spending the next month or so in terror I'd be caught.

Whether my crime was detected or not, I was never confronted. I've lost track of which painting I touched, if it still exists. The moment is barely an episode, a flicker of a brush. Yet between my certainty, until I was twelve or thirteen, that I would be a painter like my father, and my certainty now, that I am a writer like my father is a painter, stand those years when I wanted to be Stanley Kubrick instead. And in the middle of *those* years, that flicker, that sole brushstroke, stands to confess the wish to climb inside my father's hand, inside his eye and hand and brush, to clamber inside the canvases themselves and live where I couldn't help living anyway.

In my lampoon of his ambition, that earlier day on Nevins Street—my suggestion I was ready for a show—my father might have thought he heard a mouths-of-babes indictment of his own choices in dismantling so many structures of authority and order. In the appalled glance he delivered in return, maybe I glimpsed my father's regret. I at least glimpsed the ambivalence, even depression, that would for a time shade any talk of those years. The same ambivalence, I think, caused him to underrate until recently the best paintings from that chapter of his art.

But who am I to talk? I vamoosed to California, in the wake of my family's 1970s, and stayed away from Brooklyn for most of fourteen years. All that stuff I wouldn't go near in my own work, at least not directly, for most of *twenty*. Whereas my father, in 1983 or thereabouts, drew from somewhere, from who knows where, a deeper breath, and began again.

What resulted was a third phase, if that's not an inadequate name for the most sustained outpouring of his life. And, though his work in the eighties (and beyond) relies on motifs and methods developed in each of the earlier phases, and is dense with worldly emotion, it's also the most youthful. He'd earned a deeper authority, one which didn't rely on authority's noxious postures. Richard Lethem had shrugged off any last debts to Europe, and licensed himself as an American artist instead.

This flood of images opened along two avenues. First, my father replaced artist-surrogates with laborers. In *The Wall and the Worker*, from 1982, the claw hammer has come down from the studio wall, to be wielded by a carpenter slapping nails into Sheetrock. The subject's blue jeans and tool belt could be my dad's, except they might as easily be any of his partners'—Here Comes Everycontractor. In other paintings the worker dons a signature dust mask, a bit of realism which also freed the figure as an archetype: the routine handler of poisons, a wader in urban detritus. If my father had been the uneasy conscience of a gentrification, he now offered a glimpse of its underbelly. The laborer pictures were dispatches from the Gowanus Canal and Red Hook, our zone's margins, where neglect and decay had been pushed by the growth of the renovator class. Where the earlier paintings had been porous to the life of our home, he'd now opened the door to the street, and to intimations of urban strife, racial and otherwise.

The second wellspring was historical. In my father's hometown, in western Missouri, a black man named Raymond Gunn, accused of the rape and murder of a teacher, was burned alive on the roof of her one-room schoolhouse. The lynching took place the year before my father's birth; two men soon to become my uncles by marriage were, as high-school boys, at the mob's fringes. By the time my father came of age the story was a communal legend suffocated in silence. Lurking in his moral imagination, 1930s Midwestern trauma now arrived as an explicit subject in his work, as if called out by the 1970s Brooklyn trauma which had just begun proliferating there.

By now I was out of the house. First, off to college, then to my California self-exile from all things Brooklyn. My visits to my father's studio became more sporadic, more ceremonial, and kinder. I'd fly into New York to stay with friends in Manhattan, then take the subway to Brooklyn, and trudge to his new studio, under the Manhattan Bridge, often, it seemed, in fresh-fallen snow. He would give me coffee, then invite me in to consider his art.

My father allowed me to play prodigal. We became relative strangers for a while, in order to make our friendship. And I had to make myself a writer to show my father and myself some autonomy—which freed me, soon after, to confess my debt to his work. So I encountered the marvel of his eighties evolution in a sequence of punctuated equilibria. At first the variety of imagery felt anarchic. Now I grasp the sense of it all. The "worker" and "Raymond" motifs had merged. The new paintings took an accounting of American violence and sufferance, embodied in a darkly fantastical series of male figures from both the urban and the rural undergrounds of my father's imagination: circus strongmen, hospital orderlies, traveling salesmen, crypt keepers, secret agents, handymen, henchmen. They form a gallery of suspects as personal as Guston's hooded legion. These were Men with Tools, working feverishly to greet disaster with professional dignity intact, even if some of their tools were as feeble as a kite or banana, or as booby-trapped as a gun or a can of solvent. It was as if my father had adapted William Carlos Williams's dictum—"No ideas but in things"—to his turn from ivory tower to a carpenter's earthly savvy: No authority but in implements. But with the insight came the warning: dodging complicity with Establishment modes of power through violence wasn't a cinch. *Homo Faber* might also be *Homo Wrecker*.

Richard Lethem had reclaimed, from the depopulated tableaus of the sixties, his insight into the yearning gravity of inanimate objects. But, having worked from live models for ten years, his brush fixates on bodies. My father had learned a lot, by then, about community, violence, and disease, and about trying to put human flesh and human life on canvas, and discovering how it resists being put there. So every fabulation is run through what he'd found to be the bottom (and top) line: the physical absolutes of human experience. If he's a surrealist it's not the drawing-room gamesmanship of Magritte, but of Julio Cortázar and Bob Dylan and early Cormac McCarthy, where a gothic personal phantasmagoria is made necessary by an immensity of emotional response not encompassed by realist methods. The results are some of the least rarified artworks I've had the privilege to know.

Have I broken into the studio again, just to neaten up the drips? All this may be no better than a cartoon rendering, a pass with my ape's bone of language over the impossible intersection of Richard Lethem's painting and my wishful thinking. The account's not half full. Where in this is my father's passion for John Berryman's *Dream Songs*? Where's his ritual of finding workmen's gloves, abandoned in gutters, and pinning them to his studio wall, or gluing them to his canvases? His scattering of well-worn Lightning Hopkins and Elmore James cassettes, his green painting table with its molten Vesuvius pyramids of petrified colors? What's missing here is only the whole matter: my father in his studio, painting, as he has always been, as he likely is this morning. I'd only need to pick up the phone to find him there. To interrupt him, though I know he'd be glad to talk. See him: my father painting. My father painting, in a converted barn in Maine now, adjusting the space heater, stepping back from canvas to palette table to mix a color, or just to have a look, to see what he's done, to judge whether the expression on the face of that acrobat or feral goat or Tultepec god (he's been inspired by Mexican art lately) is just right, conveys the shade of greed or delight he'd intended, carrying the story just that bit further. My father in the studio in a mustard-colored sweater. My father in the studio with a mug of coffee, long since cold. My father in the studio painting. My father in his studio, pausing to read a sonnet. My father in his studio, half finishing a letter to his brother, then picking up his brush. My father, in his studio, layering act upon act, color upon color, practicing his art.

Two or Three Things

I Dunno

About Cassavetes

A man and a woman are walking out of a movie theater. They opened the paper that morning and saw that it was playing—just a single showing, at that run-down, shabby movie theater where nobody ever goes. But this was their chance, so they rushed in and bought tickets, an afternoon show on a weekday. Sat down in those broken movie-theater seats, the two of them the sole couple in the crowd. Though crowd's not the word for it, the place is empty apart from a few guys sitting by themselves, the type that go to obscure movies in run-down theaters on weekday after-noons. The man and the woman don't care, they're excited, so. Lights go down, movie plays, lights go up. Now they're walking out of the theater.

They've just watched a movie by John Cassavetes. I'd say it doesn't matter which one, but I know you know I don't mean one of the bad ones we try not to talk about, from near the beginning or near the end of his career. The man and the woman have just watched one of the great ones.

You know the movies I mean, the ones that change your life. One you never forget where you were when you saw it first or how it felt to see it, one that made you think: *What the hell was that? I need to see that again! Who is this Cassavetes?* No, they watched that one they'd heard so much about—the one about the family, the friends, the siblings, the performers, the one about the man and the woman.

"You okay?" he asked.

"Sure, yeah, I'm fine."

"Nothing wrong?"

"Nope."

"Because I couldn't help noticing there was a lot of fidgeting, squirming around in your seat, heavy sighing going on in there. So I was wondering if something was wrong."

"Okay, sure, but I'm fine, thanks, I'm great."

"So, wasn't that amazing?"

"I guess so." She gave a sort of heavy sigh now, if you were watching for that kind of thing, which he was.

"You didn't love it?"

"There were a lot of incredible things in it."

"Incredible is one word. That movie was all about my life and everything I feel."

"I was a little impatient."

"I can't fathom that and I think you were watching it wrong."

"A lot of it seemed like, I don't know, actor's exercises, these endless frenzied reiterations that don't really go anywhere."

"It made you uncomfortable."

"I love you but it made me tired."

"You resisted it."

"I love you but I'm sorry I didn't resist it."

"Well quit saying you love me because if you don't love that movie you don't love me because I am that movie, that movie is me."

"You're nothing like that movie."

"I am inside and if you could see who I really am you would know."

"Lower your voice."

"I don't have to."

"We swore no more yelling on the street."

"I'M NOT YELLING ON THE STREET I'M JUST TRYING TO UNDERSTAND HOW YOU COULD SAY THAT MOVIE WAS LIKE ACTING EXERCISES! DON'T WALK AWAY!"

"I just can't be around you right now."

"You don't need to say that please don't say that hey wait come on don't walk so fast—"

"Lady, are you okay?" The guy who says this, a large guy who must have been in the doorway of the restaurant, is upon them so quickly they're both startled and jostle into each other as they halt. The woman pushes herself away from the collision and stumbles for a second and the large guy steps between the man and the woman and puts his hand up like a traffic cop and says again, "You okay?" The woman just shakes her head, no, yes, keeps walking. Big guy walks with her. Man stands watching, arms outstretched though nobody's seeing him, well, maybe loads of people, now that he's bothered to notice that the whole street's full of gawking faces—they were never alone—but not the woman or the big guy she's walking with. Those two, they just keep going.

I'm thinking about minor characters in the films of John Cassavetes. Take McCarthy, played by Val Avery, in *Faces*. McCarthy's the one who's trying to get over with Jeannie (played by John Cassavetes's wife, Gena Rowlands) when Richard (played by John Marley) shows up. He's the guy who admits to Jeannie, the tender call girl, that he's baffled by his own son, a six-foot Dartmouth man in tennis shoes.

Faces is in one sense nothing more than a flash-frozen record of the condition of the marriage of its two main characters: Richard and his wife, Maria (played by Lynn Carlin). The film presents Richard's night away from home, and what Maria does while he's away. In another sense, *Faces* is a voracious ribald mugging of its viewers' defensive assumptions: assumptions about how much a film is allowed to make them feel about men and women and daily life, about the expression or suppression of passionate impulses in a marriage or in a house or in a nightclub or in America in 1965. It's also a shattering formal essay in compression and explosion, a mix of sensory overload ("I dream of Jeannie with the light brown hair! I dream of Jeannie with the light brown hair! I! Dream! Of! Jeannie! With! The! Light! Brown! Hair!" chanted, sung and bellowed by the characters until you wish to scream) and deprivation: deprivation of the ordinary consolations available to audience members, who find themselves wrenched into bewildering complicity, forced to stumble in the reeling footprints of the seemingly intoxicated performers.

In the middle of all this, mistaking himself for a player, is poor McCarthy. The guy just wants a night out. Wants, as it will happen, something he can't quite put his finger on, nor can we, but it comes in the package of Gena Rowlands. And McCarthy doesn't have any inkling he's not the main point here. Eyeballs bulging with need and its denial, teeth bared in sardonic self-loathing, he's gonna get what he wants if it kills him, if it would kill him even to name it. In fact, we can see that Jeannie's already halfway promised herself to Richard, that she's readying herself for a rendezvous with Richard even as she wriggles out of McCarthy's grasp.

When McCarthy and Richard face one another it will be with the horror of mutual recognition, a doppelgänger dream out of Poe or Nabokov: two married guys, two businessmen, mirrored even in their acne scars (and how rare, that facial confession of adolescence, for an actor! How specific that this director chose two pockmarked guys for these parts!). Only their respective styles of brokenhearted swagger distinguish them, only hair-splitting degrees of difference in the hierarchy of the suburban damned.

But Richard's still offstage, and McCarthy figures he's the star of the show. Indeed, he's given an episode of such merciless poignancy that he nearly steals the movie: McCarthy has blundered his way into Jeannie's boudoir. He and Jeannie have left behind in the living room another couple, who carry on with the insane cavorting which has dominated the film to this point, the rituals of drink and song which seem a barely sufficient stand-in for all human yearning, for sex and conversation, possibly for food and air and water. But McCarthy wants more. He wants contact. And he's granted it, contact and a bit of grace, even. Jeannie embraces him in tender silence as he spills it out: "Oh, boy, what a life . . . what have I got after all these years? A big house, a kooky wife, and a kid who wears sneakers. I like you, Jeannie. I want you to like me for myself, I'd like to make love to you and know that you like me for my charm, my wit . . .'"

Jeannie says nothing. Nuzzles him slightly. Her gift of listening is what she's got for him. It'll do, barely. McCarthy has by now gathered that she's not lending him more than an ear, tonight. So he wrenches himself out of the sacred moment, back into the living room, back into the drunken whirl—but not before disheveling his own hair and untucking his shirt to simulate the grope scene he's ashamed wasn't unfolding behind those closed doors. He's showing off for his buddy and the second girl, pretending he scored, at the small expense of whatever shreds of Jeannie's respect he hasn't already torched.

McCarthy, though minor, isn't half done yet. When Richard shows up, McCarthy'll insult him, put him in a headlock, and then forge a wheedling, backslapping, faux friendship with him even as Jeannie's kicking McCarthy and his friend and the other girl out the door. I'm going to leave McCarthy here, though, where I treasure him most, prepping himself in the mirror on his way out of Jeannie's bedroom, mussing his hair, putting on a boorish jocularity to protect himself from himself, from his confession of sensitivity. If you're like me, you love him. That's the mystery: I don't find I want to push McCarthy any harder than he's pushed himself. I want to console the guy.

"Conversation!" Nick Longhetti, played by Peter Falk, commands of his houseguests in *A Woman Under the Influence*. "Weather! Ordinary conversation!" He's howling like an impotent Prospero in the storm of liquefied emotion that is his family's life, begging for a taste of the small talk or pleasantry he imagines will vouchsafe the normality—and sustainability—of his domestic arrangement. (Another day at the same table, when he and his co-workers share a spaghetti dinner, he attempts to plug the gap himself with an anecdote so inept that it verges on poetry: "You go for months, you don't see any kids, suddenly you see strollers, kids everywhere. Must be something in the air.")

Nick, fighting the evidence that his wife, Mabel (Gena Rowlands), presents in every vibrant, paradoxical, absurdly responsive cell of her body, can't accept that life is so fundamentally up for grabs, that one moment tumbles upon the next with no sense of accountability to its predecessor, that every social code is up for constant renegotiation, like the stakes at a poker table where the dealer's called a game of infinity card draw. But also, Mabel sleeps with other guys. This is, weirdly, one of the least remarked-upon aspects of this much remarked-upon film: Mabel sleeps around. We can dwell endlessly on the ambiguities of Mabel's and Nick's distress yet somehow flinch from the brunt of Nick's rage at betrayal. Just when these films have taught us to distrust the obvious, they'll tease us for overlooking it.

So maybe Nick's our surrogate, we in our disorientation and dismay at the uncertainties into which Mabel's directorial style (of her marriage, of her children's after-school parties, of the expressions that cross her face) and Cassavetes's directorial style (of his movie, of his actress wife) have thrust us. Except, as a surrogate, Nick stinks. He's crazy too. He's screwed it all up, failing to call Mabel and simply tell her he's stuck working all night and will miss their marital "date" (in preparation for which the kids have been shipped off to his mother-in-law's). Boorish at best, Nick seems incapable of soothing speech, and instead displays a fondness for jolting Mabel with Popeyeish outbursts. We yearn, as viewers, to leap through the screen and throttle him more times than we can count. So whose side are we on? Those poor kids? Is that how little foothold we've got here?

I'm thinking about a minor character in the films of John Cassavetes, a minor character who may in fact be the star (even if he sometimes, in the history of the reception of the movies, declined to show up): the viewer of the films. Cassavetes mostly wrecks ordinary systems of cinematic identification with his characters. On the technical level, this means the near-total avoidance of point-of-view shots, which, traditionally, form the primary language of alliance between viewer and screen actor. In terms of tone, a refusal to commit to comedy or tragedy, faux realism or absurdist farce. In terms of the presentation of the material itself, he withholds those reassuring cues usually given to privilege a character as worthy of our sympathy, and charming enough for us to want to hang out with—the confirming glances of irascible and deferential character actors, the petting of the heads of dogs and babies, the outlines of a reliably beguiling persona. Even more dismaying, at times he withholds vast (yet easily divulged) realms of pure information: who's married and not, who's whose brother or sister, whether or not someone's a girlfriend or a prostitute, or what the outcome of a fundamentally worrisome event (worksite accident, shooting, one-night stand) might have been. The preference is to keep the viewer on his or her cognitive heels, boxing with a flurry of contradictory material.

The paradox of Cassavetes's style is that while he appears to wreck identification in this way he somehow creates a vocabulary of cinematic experiences impossible to describe except as "personal," "emotional," and "indulgent." Despite the frustrating blockage of our sympathies, nobody's ever slandered the work as *cold*, *distant*, or *objective*. What Cassavetes has done, rather than wreck identification, is to *displace* it, to an unspecified place somewhere in the Bermuda Triangle between viewer, the viewer's expectations and beliefs as to what the film ought to be doing, and Cassavetes's own implied presence as director. Anecdotes from Cassavetes's sets endlessly underline his own personal presence—his beckoning, cackling, tearful bodily presence behind the lens, often just inches from his performers. His sound men routinely had to erase his own voice from the soundtracks, where he'd intruded in exhorting and provoking the actors. So the exhilarating ultimatum Cassavetes presents is to invest so deeply in his own perilously negotiated viewpoint (as witness, catalyst, exorcist, as grumbling parent and conspiratorial sibling to his actors) that we're forced to abandon the maps and protractors we'd not even noticed we ordinarily keep between us and an encounter with a film. If this is a poker game, we're not even sure we can see Cassavetes's cards, or our own, as we're asked to place our bet.

We resort to Charlie Parker, the blues, jazz, beatnik poetry, "If you have to ask, you'll never know," Miles Davis with his back to the audience

(Tom Charity: "There's a correlation with Bebop here. Like Charlie Parker and Miles Davis, Cassavetes could take a standard tune and turn it inside out . . ."), Jackson Pollock, Norman Mailer's *White Negro*, and the cult of "hip," all the restless-in-the-fifties romanticism that can seem in retrospect so mannered and indulgent but was in the context of its moment an act, an acting out, likely as necessary as a drowning man's thrashing to the surface for a gulp of air. If the word *uptight* had never existed, and the world to which it alludes was unrecorded elsewhere, the fabulous evidence of the many species of *uptighteosity* catalogued in *Faces* alone would make the term a necessary invention of social historians wishing to decipher the consciousness of the middle of America's last century.

Cassavetes is film's Bob Dylan. I mean, it: *Faces* is his "Like a Rolling Stone." Both of those artworks make a cascading, exuberant attack on the certainties of the audience, both consist of a declaration of revulsion, by the authors, of their subjects ("Miss Lonely" in the Dylan, and Richard and Maria in *Faces*), one which evolves, uncannily, into a declaration of freedom and renewed possibility on those same subjects' devastated behalves. And both were delivered in the spirit of a deliberate formal blasphemy (by use of excessive length—of scene, and song—and excessive force, excessive bile) against the formats intended, in their day, to contain them.

What's more, the "social criticism" that underlies both *Faces* and *Shadows*—a social criticism that, as we can see from the more or less contemporaneous art of Richard Yates, Jack Kerouac, Ken Nordine, and the Fugs, was an almost automatic creative response to the American fifties—was as inessential, ultimately, to Cassavetes's art as "protest" singing is to Dylan's music, *but equally essential in the development of that art*. By inscribing provocation as the footing for a relationship with their audience, both Dylan and Cassavetes evolve through social criticism into a vocabulary of emotional defiance, of stances of provocation turned inward.

To go on listing similarities, both Dylan and Cassavetes derive energy from claiming (dubious) membership in a minority of sensitive outsiders, an existentialist identity far more elusive to define than merely "hip," "avant-garde," or "leftist." In making this claim, both of them alien-ated doctrinaire former supporters like Jonas Mekas, self-appointed guardian of avant-garde film authenticity, and *Sing Out!* magazine and Pete Seeger, self-appointed guardian of protest folk-song authenticity. Both rely on confusing or surprising their artistic collaborators with sud-den reassignments (key changes, new pages in the script) in order to overcome recording mediums which tend to freeze out spontaneity. Even the song that plays in the final scene of *Faces*, Charlie Smalls's "Never Felt Like This Before," could be seen as a rough draft of Dylan's indictment: "How does it feeuull?" or "Ballad of a Thin Man": "Something is happen-ing here / But you don't know what it is / Do you, Mister Jones?"

John Cassavetes, a writer, crafted language as exacting and persuasive (and funny) in its musical irrationality, its disguised artifice, as anything by Stephen Dixon, Grace Paley, or Don DeLillo ("What did you eat, Ma? You ate fish at Hamburger Heaven? Why would you do that?"). But the films evade capture in nets of language, and, sometimes, in their charac-ters' inarticulateness, seem *anti*-verbal. Try watching with the picture off: as a purely acoustic experience, *Faces* is pure gibberish and singsong— compulsive unfunny jokes, distorted repetitive song fragments, and hideously banal male pecking-order riffs. The meaning is in the faces themselves, and the stances of the bodies as they reel through these hall-ways, stances of grief and longing the jokes cover and the bodies uncover. On closer inspection, though, the gibberish is pierced, as if electrified, by lines so nakedly the vessels of pain ("I want a divorce!" or "I thought you were supposed to be saving my life") that the characters shouldn't be able to walk or breathe after uttering them, let alone pull the tab on another can of beer and resume their songs.

This is Beckett or Pinter stuff, really. But the material arises out of a laboratory of actorly and photographic experimentation, and is suffused with a fondness for homely gestures of hesitation, of embarrassment. So the craft disguises itself as happenstance disclosure. Though we know better, a part of us thinks it's all an accident, a documentary glimpse. The artists here have invaded their own privacy, we think, as they invade ours.

The same thing that makes it possible for some people to loathe Cassavetes's actors (and therefore the director who has revealed them to us) causes others of us to sentimentally patronize them in our adoration: They're too vulnerable to be acting!

We project that same vulnerability onto Cassavetes as an artist when we hesitate to discuss his limitations or compromises, as though he were some species of animal, a beautiful and tender freak set loose in our brutal human world. We kid ourselves that we're not good enough for him, which becomes a convenient opportunity to refuse to meet him totally. If we can laugh at Orson Welles for his wine commercials and *The Muppet Movie*, why do we wince at the mention of Cassavetes's participation in *Big Trouble* or *Whose Life Is It Anyway?* It's as though we're hurting Cassavetes by knowing he lived in the world too. Really, we're seeking safety for ourselves. By holding him in a special category, we quarantine the disturbance he provokes in us by thinking it a report from an exotic, who speaks to us through the gates of a preserve given names like "The Sixties" or "Bohemia" or "Cassavetes-land" (John Voight: "Cassavetes is a place"). At worst, the films can be taken as a childish vote for a "freer way of life" as easy to endorse as it is impossible or undesirable to embody.

Then again, what artist have I ever met *totally?* How did that become my insane standard for this art? *J'accuse*: Cassavetes is implicated in this. By advertising his artworks, in interview after interview, as an ongoing act of human exploration, he raised the stakes of its reception to intolerance of anything but utter rejection or devotion. Furthermore, he did so, cleverly, without claiming to have accomplished anything definite: no certainty of the value of the result, only of the project of *attempting* the result. ("We're making a picture about the inner life and nobody really believes that it can be put on the screen, including me, I don't believe it either, but screw it.") The films scream: *Believe or leave, but don't make me justify myself!* This may just be a way of saying, again, that Cassavetes loaded the stakes between his audience and his films, much as he loaded them between his actors and his material (forcing them to work without coherent instruction in order to throw them into their own emotional resources), and between himself and the sponsors of and collaborators in his directing career (by shooting vast amounts of footage, including scenes he'd probably never intend to use, then editing versions of the films that were five and eight hours long, and by offering and then withdrawing versions that were more "entertaining," in favor of final cuts that were more ambiguous or confrontational, and by creating enemies of critics, financiers, and talk-show hosts). Peter Bogdanovich: "He wanted to be in a struggle."

It's easy to be dissatisfied by other movies after watching Cassavetes's, and to wish other filmmakers had Cassavetes's adamancy, his rigor, his fluency, his generosity. Yet I think it's a mistake to think all films ought to be like Cassavetes's, or to imagine that the films would retain the meaning we cherish without their real-world context of indifference by the majority of viewers or potential followers (and in truth I'm often pained to see traces of his actual influence in the work of other filmmakers).

To speak of form: Do I want to live in a world where every songwriter wants to be Bob Dylan, or every story writer wants to be Raymond Carver or Donald Barthelme (those two different versions of Cassavetean purity: Carver's authenticity through austerity, Barthelme's freedom through silliness)? As it happens, because music is less technically resistant to Dylan's innovations, and prose less resistant to Carver's and Barthelme's, than film is to Cassavetes's, I've come closer to living in those worlds than I have to a world where every filmmaker wants to be John Cassavetes. And on that basis I'd have to say, thanks but no thanks. These freak-geniuses derive their energy and meaning from their commitment to excesses which would become limitations in other hands. They, and Cassavetes, need a world of more typical art the way a shadow needs a wall.

To speak of content: If the world were as Cassavetes and his films sometimes seem to imply it simply ought to be—if everyone lived with utter freedom, like Chet in *Faces*, or if our relationships were all as giddily counterclockwise as Mabel Longhetti's—would Cassavetes's films even need to exist? Or, maybe I should ask, *could* they? I doubt it, because the world of emotion and impulse needs ground to stand on, and every provocation needs its Mr. Jones, just as every bully needs a victim (Cassavetes: "I feel that the world is very chicken. By chicken I mean that the world is too tight." Dylan: "The sun's not yellow, it's chicken"). We all may sometimes wish to be Mabel Longhetti, but how much do we actually want to be married to her?

Anyway, to ratify only those kooky characters is to overlook the pensiveness in a film like *The Killing of a Chinese Bookie*, with Ben Gazzara's infinitely self-abnegated image of the artist, or of *Husbands*, for all its apparent indulgence of boozy jollity the saddest and least-resolved of the films, or of *Opening Night*, that masterpiece of dissatisfaction. Characters like *Killing's* Cosmo Vitelli and *Opening Night's* Myrtle Gordon are people capable of failing to connect or inspire, people capable of inducing and experiencing disappointment, possibly even boredom. If we're going to give ourselves entirely to Cassavetes's work, we'd better find a way to be willing to be disappointed in it, and to disappoint it. Sometimes I want to watch something else.

I'm thinking of the minorest minor characters in the films of John Cassavetes, those dented souls littering the edges of the stories. Some of these are given unforgettably colorful turns (and names), like Zelmo Swift, the obnoxious, bellowing suitor in *Minnie and Moskowitz* (played by the same Val Avery that incarnated McCarthy, in *Faces*), or Billy Tidrow (played by Leon Wagner), the hapless victim of Mabel's excessive adoration at her spaghetti dinner, the one guest at her table who can't sing, no matter how much she exhorts him.

The Zelmo and Billy sequences, though those characters are apparently damaged by their encounters with Cassavetes's protagonists, are endearing. Others are more disturbing. I'm thinking of Eddie (Charles Horvath), the American Indian construction worker in *A Woman Under the Influence*. Eddie has the misfortune of getting in the middle of Nick Longhetti's bad mood on the construction site the day after Nick has Mabel committed to the booby hatch; he's sent tumbling down a sandy grade by Nick, whose hand on a guide rope has been made unsteady by his rage. We learn that in the fall Eddie has broken "every bone in his body," though when we see him back at work, six months later, he's more or less intact. (By the way, how has anyone ever gotten away with calling these films "plotless"?) You could miss it on first viewing, but there's a whole Eddie-the-Indian movie tucked inside *Woman*: Eddie's the same one that Mabel kicks out of her kitchen, and Eddie's wife is the one who calls Nick "a shit" when he's invited the whole gang over to welcome his wife home from her institutionalization. Finally, Billy Tidrow and Eddie sit morosely together on the steps of a trailer as Nick rounds up the rest of the construction workers for his party. Eddie and Billy have become the sole abstainers from the nutty cavalcade, having had enough of Mabel and Nick both, no matter what anyone else thinks.

Lenny (Leonard P. Geer), in *Love Streams*, might be my candidate for the most subtle example of this genre of character: Cassavetes's incidental roadkills. Here, Sarah Lawson (Gena Rowlands again), in a gesture of severely bizarre empathy, buys her brother Robert Harmon (Cassavetes himself) a household menagerie of pets, acquiring them in one swoop: a batch of chickens, ducks, goats, and miniature horses. She also buys a dog—Jim the dog, he's called. Jim's got a caretaker, a human friend named Lenny, and Jim and Lenny are plainly inseparable, the deepest of cross-species friends. We feel no doubt they shouldn't be parted. But Sarah buys Jim the dog. Suffering a divorce herself, she berefts Lenny of his canine pal. Lenny, like Zelmo, like Billy and Eddie, may stand for Cassavetes's awareness of the sometimes bruising nature of a brush with charisma, possibly even his own, however eccentric and well-intentioned.

I'm thinking, at last, about the characters in the Cassavetes films who may be the hardest to think about clearly, because they swim shrouded in our moonish affection, and yet also strike us as suspicious: those played by Cassavetes himself. I think it's no mistake that Cassavetes distrusted himself as an actor, and that we distrust him too. The two films which tend to persuade Cassavetes skeptics, and which strike devotees as "most perfect" (and the best entry point for newcomers), are two in which Cassevetes doesn't appear, even for a frame: *Faces* and *Woman*. The films in which he's got the biggest roles are more problematic, and usually only favorites of the already converted: *Husbands* and *Love Streams*. Cassavetes casts himself if not as a villain, then largely as a person of dangerous charm and reserve, one who indulges in the feints and masks that other, more heroically Cassavetean characters usually try to see through and strip away. If the films are a long war on self-congratulation, the characters Cassavetes plays are losers, barricaded by guile from what matters most, facing questions they've made themselves too clever or persuasive to answer.

But Cassavetes was maybe too prone to easy binaries in his rhetoric of *free versus constricted*, or *spontaneous versus rehearsed*. Beginning with *Shadows*, with its explicit study of the racial politics of bohemia, the films could be lampooned as a kind of valentine to an "other," more fluent and deep than you, or me, or himself. He's been praised as "the most color-blind of directors," but that takes the bait, again, of thinking Cassavetes a kind of *natural* or *accidental* artist, when we've agreed to know how fiercely deliberate he was, and never more so than in his casting. To me, then, the blackness of the girlfriends disappointed by Ben Gazzara's character in *Chinese Bookie* and by John Cassavetes's character in *Love Streams* is anything but color-blind. It's at least as specific as John Marley's acne scars. By pairing black women with these men who are both surrogates for himself and studies in tragic reserve, he's surely driving at something. Unless we believe the choice is guilty overcompensation on Cassavetes's part, it's an analysis of a guilty overcompensation on the part of those characters—right?

Speaking of which, here's Eddie the, er, Native American, in *A Woman Under the Influence*, who has every bone in his body broken by the immigrant Italian guy. And, in the same movie, George Mortenson, Mabel's father, declines an offer of dinner with irrational fury: "I'm just *not* a spaghetti man!" Am I wrong to hear in the scene an undertone of Wasp revulsion (Spaghetti/Longhetti), as though what Mortenson really wants to say is *if my blond daughter hadn't married a Wop maybe she wouldn't be so fucking crazy*? What's more, Seymour Moskowitz, the unworthy suitor of the Waspy Minnie Moore in *Minnie and Moskowitz*, is Jewish.

Cassavetes's shifty racial allegories are everywhere, when we begin to look.

But the deepest binary is, of course, men and women. In both *Husbands* and *Faces* Cassavetes invented his unique language of behavior in part by matching professional male actors with unprofessional females, in order to emphasize the uncertainty and "naturalness" of the women in contrast to the confident, slick, and rehearsed styles of the men. In *Shadows*, in a similar gambit, Anthony Ray was shown pages of dialogue weeks in advance, while Leila Goldoni was only handed them on the morning of the shoot. So: Are women more "natural" than men? Or is it just that imbalances in our society dictate the appearance of that difference? Again, we have to agree that Cassavetes was either making a deep interrogation into his material, or not. But he's not innocent.

This is the cause, then, of my fascination with the parts Cassavetes played himself: the questions he never fully answered beat like a pulse in the male characters most easily taken for his stand-ins. I'm thinking of the chance that the purloined letter of Cassavetes's lifework is his own terror of boredom and superficiality, right there at the locus of so much vitality and inspiration, at the center of so much "being around him was like being in a Cassavetes movie" malarkey. I'm not accusing his beloved friends and collaborators of being sycophantic, only suggesting that he was, at the end of the day, both The Director and an enormously charming and manipulative guy, the kind who caused others to feel lucky to have been manipulated.

In other words, the only actor in a Cassavetes film who doesn't have the privilege of being directed by, disarmed and charmed and embarrassed and transmuted by the direction of John Cassavetes, of being *called on his shit* by John Cassavetes, is John Cassavetes. His character's goodbye wave at the end of *Love Streams* has been seen as a dying man's farewell to his audience, but that character's isolation in the final shot strikes me as more than a little like Humphrey Bogart's at the end of *In a Lonely Place* (one of the most Cassavetean films in the classical Hollywood cinema): barred in a prison of his own personality, watching a last chance at life walk out the door. Maybe Cassavetes cast himself as a man of ingenious and tragic masks because he felt like he was getting away with something.

I'm thinking of the not-entirely-minor character in my life of the woman who took me to my first Cassavetes movie. I was about to turn thirty, and my first novel was about to be published. I liked to think of myself as having already completed my basic education in film, and, as a writer much influenced by film, as having long since assembled my array of primary influences. (I still like to think of myself that way. I was so much older then, I'm older than that now.) She was only in her early twenties, but she knew to drag me to see *Faces*, at the Red Vic, on Haight Street in San Francisco. She'd already seen it, and was wordless with excitement. I wanted an explanation in advance, having heard that the Cassavetes films were *nothing more than a series of actor's exercises*, but she refused to offer one.

It knocked me out, of course. I left the movie theater wrestling with what seemed then to me to be an overwhelming insight, though from this vantage it appears to be not much more than the first level of resistance peeling away from what would become my consuming obsession with Cassavetes's films: that life had been revealed to be so much more like a series of actor's exercises than I'd ever understood before. This epiphany seemed to me profound enough that I knew I would have to change my life, or at least my art, to account for it.

It was sometime in this period that the same woman broke up with her boyfriend and, in the process, made an obscure gesture in which I became faintly implicated: she took his television and VCR hostage and hid them in my apartment. I remember using them to watch Preston Sturges's *Unfaithfully Yours* (another Cassavetean film, come to think of it). Presently the woman and her ex-boyfriend reached an accord, on terms unknown to me, and she collected the television and VCR and returned them to him.

I'm thinking of one last story concerning this woman. When, a few months later, my first novel was published, she wanted me to know how excited she was for me. So she told me a story: she'd seen my novel for sale in a bookstore, also on Haight Street, one of the few places that was carrying the book. I asked if she'd read it. No, she explained. In her excitement for me she'd attempted to shoplift it—had gotten it into her purse, and gotten herself halfway out the door—and then been caught, reprimanded, and let go. Now she was ashamed to go back to the bookstore. She left it at that, but she knew—and I knew she knew I knew—it was the most flattering story she could tell me.

The Beards

(a coda)

The Heavenly Music Corporation
(1980–82, mom dead)

No Pussyfooting is an album by the guitar player Robert Fripp and the keyboard player Brian Eno. The album consists of two songs, or compositions: there are no voices on the record, no lyrics. Unlike other recordings by Fripp or Eno, alone or as members of groups, *No Pussyfooting* doesn't consist of studio overdubs, of layers of sound. Though the music provides a richness, a sense of intricacy, the two cuts appear to be long improvisations between the players, conducted in real time, within simple parameters. Side one consists of achingly long tones, swells of sound that rise and fade. In vocal terms, the instruments groan or wail. They keen. On side two, the tones are frantic with ripples, oscillations. In vocal terms, the instruments ululate. Or orgasm.

Side one is called "The Heavenly Music Corporation." Side two, "Swastika Girls."

I bought *No Pussyfooting* in 1979 or 1980, at the record store on the eighth floor of Abraham and Straus, a palatial department store on

Fulton Street, a few blocks from where I lived. My friend Jeremy and I had been going there regularly to browse the long sections of Frank Zappa and Kinks records, and to dare ourselves to spend money on some of the mysterious products we couldn't have investigated otherwise. I was curious about Brian Eno because he was the producer of the newest Talking Heads record. I imagine I selected the two Eno records I bought—*Taking Tiger Mountain (By Strategy)* and *No Pussyfooting*—on the strength of their jacket art, which was alluringly dark and strange, and which had a resemblance to "gallery" art, as did the jackets of Talking Heads albums.

I also liked Eno's name. It sounded vaguely alien, bliplike, like those of some of the writers I'd begun to idolize, partly for the distance from the prosaic seemingly encoded in their surnames: Lem, Kafka, Poe, Borges.

When I got those records home, *Taking Tiger Mountain (By Strategy)* turned out to be a sequence of songs in conventional rock format, three to six minutes long, mostly with guitars and drums underlying creepy, synthesized sound effects and ominous, gnomic lyrics. Perfect, in other words. *No Pussyfooting* was this other thing: a pair of fuzzy electronic suites, which absolutely refused to beguile. I should have filed it in my collection and forgotten it, gravely disappointed, as I'd imagine most of its teenage buyers were. Instead, I decided I loved "The Heavenly Music Corporation," and hated "Swastika Girls." The first was, as its name suggested, deeply soothing, the long tones invoking surrender and contemplation. The other was compulsive, boiling, and its name offered a couple of reasons I ought to be intimidated by it.

I had a room to myself, on the top floor of our house. My bed was on a loft, built above a hivelike construction of desktops and storage spaces. Directly below where I placed my pillow was a wooden compartment which neatly held my amplifier and turntable. I had a set of headphones—absurdly heavy, ear-clamping muffs, connected to the stereo by a mushy, coiled, rubber-coated cord, twice as thick as a telephone's.

Late at night, when I was done reading, and had shut off my light, I'd wear the headphones and listen to the twenty-one minutes of "The Heavenly Music Corporation," or as much as I could before it lulled me to sleep. I memorized each aching swell of guitar and synth, anticipating the moment when the synthesizer's repeated plunge toward a certain note suddenly seems to persuade the guitar to follow, so that the second half of the piece becomes a long finishing, an ebbing away.

Some nights, whatever teenage anxiety or fear thrilled my body kept me awake through the whole piece. In that case I'd lean over the edge of my bed, still wearing the headphones, and place the needle at the start of the track again. I'd mastered an art of nudging the monstrous phones off my head as I launched into deeper stages of sleep, so I'd wake to find them crammed into the margin between my mattress and the wall, yet never recalled dislodging them.

"The Heavenly Music Corporation" was a secret friend who flattered my wishes both to vibrate to the universe's pulse in some post-human sense, through the exclusion of banal seductions of language or melody, and to align with esoteric art, made by freaks from a pop-art future, beyond the ken of my teachers or family. Truthfully, I was using it as a white-noise generator, like the one I recently learned a jittery friend employs to put himself to sleep. But Fripp's long guitar solo was also a human voicing I grew to know better, probably, than its maker. His on-the-spot thinking, audible as he tested the surf of Eno's synthesizer, was like a morality only I understood. I covered it in sleep, then bore it out into the day with me, a surrogate brainwave with which to reply to the world.

The Man Who Fell to Earth
(1976, mom out of hospital)

My mother and her boyfriend took me to a midday showing of the Nicholas Roeg film *The Man Who Fell to Earth* at the Quad Cinema on Thirteenth Street in Manhattan. *The Man Who Fell to Earth* is a surrealist science-fiction movie full of gorgeous hallucinatory photography. It stars David Bowie as a gentle and moody alien visitor to our planet, one who, upon encountering man's inhumanity to aliens, becomes increasingly bitter and self-loathing, until he ends up a decadent and drunken pop star. This was the bowdlerized American release, missing the blatant sex scenes which have since been restored, though David Bowie's attempt to present his "true self" to his human lover, played by Candy Clark— shedding disguises, he reveals goatlike slit pupils, and a smooth, doll-like bump in place of his genitals—was shocking to me.

As we three stepped back out into the daylight of Manhattan I was deeply in the spell of the film. It was my first experience meeting a brand-new cultural artifact calibrated perfectly to my private symbolic vocabulary, which was already fairly well formed. I'd been reading Ray Bradbury's *Martian Chronicles* and a handful of other classic science-fiction stories, and *alien equals alienated* was a rebus I grasped. *Any one of these people I see walking around me*, I remember thinking, in astonishment, as we made our way back to the subway, *could be like him*. By "like him" I meant, or thought I meant: a secret visitor from another planet. But my wonder at the film was really at the force of my identification with the figure of the misunderstood alien, and I didn't imagine for a minute that I wasn't an earthling. So what I really meant was: Any one of these people I see walking around me could be like *me*. Could feel like me, just as I felt like Bowie. That is to say: subjective, sad, and special.

Barry Lyndon
(1975, mom undiagnosed)

My father lived in a commune. According to my parents' arrangement, my brother and sister and I spent two days a week there. The oldest child on the premises, I systematically made friends with the adults, finding points of common interest with each of them. Libby and her family lived in the commune too. Libby was a mother of two children, and she and her husband were drifting apart. Libby and I decided we were the only two people in the world who understood the greatness of Stanley Kubrick's rejected historical saga *Barry Lyndon*, and so we went to see it a second time, just us. Libby drove us out to Bay Ridge to find the one theater in Brooklyn still showing it, a cavernous old emporium likely soon to be sliced into a three- or four-plex.

Barry Lyndon is an epic of merciless slowness, an account of human vanity and corruption charted in microscopic degrees. The film is lucid, unhysterical, purged of deference to the suffering of its characters.

Instead, the narrative posture is of droll tolerance for human failings. *This is so great*, I remember thinking as I sat and watched it in perfect silence beside Libby. This is so great, this is so great, this is so great, this is so great. *Barry Lyndon* offers an amplitude of emptiness—as much as *2001: A Space Odyssey*, it takes as its ultimate subject, the ocean of space which surrounds each human life, and isolates each from any other. Into this space I fit the fierce certainty of my response: *This is so, so great.*

Wish You Were Here
(1979 or 1980, mom dead)

The party was in the apartment of a man named Louis, who wore his hair in Rastafarian-style dreadlocks, and whose shelves were full of paperback science fiction of the saga variety—Frank Herbert's *Dune* books, and Philip José Farmer's *Riverworld*. In the middle of the living room stood a hookah, surrounded by low cushions. I'd been inhaling marijuana from one of the tubes of the hookah, a surprisingly easy thing to do quite a lot of. And I'd been feeling very much a part of this delightful party, which consisted entirely of adults, men and women in their twenties, all of whom seemed to have accepted me as a given in their circle, despite the fact that I'd never been to Louis's apartment before, and many of the people there were strangers.

Yet I wasn't mistaken. This mutual comfort extended from the degree to which I'd been adopted into the company of my grown-up friend Michael, who ran a used bookstore on Atlantic Avenue, a few blocks from my home. It also spoke to Michael's charismatic influence on his friends, a clan of actors and hippies loosely centered around Michael and a couple of his best friends from Queens, where he'd grown up. I'd wandered into Michael's shop one day, attracted not only by the used books which had already become my passion but by the oddness of a ramshackle enterprise which surely reminded me of my parents' milieu. For, improbably, the bookstore on Atlantic was also a puppet theater, and the home office of a small, informal moving company, each in partnership with Michael's friend Larry.

I made myself an immediate sidekick to Michael and Larry, and insisted on apprenticing myself in all three of the trades they ran from the single storefront. I painted backdrops and collected receipts at the puppet shows (I also rounded up local kids to help make an audience). I joined on small moving jobs, more than once mooring the guide rope on a block and tackle as we shifted a couch through the upstairs window of a Brooklyn apartment. And I immersed myself in Michael's bookselling knowledge. This was the beginning of the only trade I've ever practiced—it was by working in used bookstores that I supported myself for twelve years after dropping out of college. Before long I opened the shop by myself, on those days when Michael didn't feel like making the trip from his Upper East Side Manhattan apartment. I was apprenticed to Michael as a reader too, aping his interests in John Cowper Powys, Colin Wilson, and Thomas Berger, and I took home my pay from the shop in books, not cash. When we differed—Michael found Borges trite—I was ashamed. When I succeeded in seeding Michael's interest, as I did in the case of Philip K. Dick, I exulted.

It was in the shop, then, that Michael's friends got to taking the presence of his fifteen-year-old acolyte for granted. Nevertheless, I must have seemed a bit adrift that night, on my pillow at the hookah, grinning and smiling at the women in the room, trying to follow or perhaps insert myself into nearby conversations. I'd inhaled more pot than I ever had before, more than I realized. So Bob, another of Michael's friends, made a small intervention.

Bob was a tall, elegant black man, an actor and a jazz musician—a trumpet player and scat singer, to be exact. My first memory of Bob was at Michael's shop, as he burst in one day to report on his audition for a part in a jazz musical. Bob had come straight from the audition, which, according to his account to Michael and me, he'd bungled. "I went like this—" Bob said, and began to reproduce his inept scat singing for us. "I mean, all I had to do was this—" Now he scatted beautifully. "But instead I was going—" Again, he reproduced the crappy scat singing. "I could have just—" Now it was good again. Michael laughed knowingly. I might have laughed too, but I was spellbound. Bob's ability to make me hear the difference in formal pressure behind a successful improvisation and a failed one still stands as one of the finest aesthetic lessons I've ever grabbed on the go. At the time, the self-reproaching magnetism of his impromptu exhibition made me think it impossible he wouldn't get the part. How could anyone else have been as wonderful?

This night, at Louis's party, Bob had seen something in my eyes as I sat at the hookah which made him wish if not to rescue then to divert me. He tapped me on my spaced-out shoulder and made me follow him to Louis's bedroom. There he sat me on the edge of the bed and placed a pair of heavy headphones on my ears.

"Listen to this," he said.

"What?" I said.

"Just listen."

Bob pressed a button on a cassette deck. The music that flooded my ears was sensual, ominous, and infinitely protracted, oceanic. The record was Pink Floyd's *Wish You Were Here*, which begins with the band's fourteen-minute "Shine on You Crazy Diamond, Part I–V," a suite I'd later discover was a tribute to their former bandmate, Syd Barrett, lost to drugs and schizophrenia at the end of the sixties. The album is recorded for stereo with such pinpoint hallucinatory clarity that its effect on headphones, in my stoned condition, was to suggest I'd plunged out of a landscape of two aural dimensions into one of three, or five, or twenty. I felt able to place each of the notes in a precise place in the air before my eyes, to watch them flicker and vanish like embers.

He'd given a gift. It was as though Bob had said: *Jonathan, the time for you to pretend you are an adult among adults is through for the night. You're a charming kid and we like you very much, but the strain is showing. So, quit pretending you understand things you only half understand, and return yourself to wonderment, to masturbation, to dreaming.* That set of songs, met for the first time on headphones and marijuana, would have reduced anyone to a childlike state. So there was no shame for me in sitting alone there, entranced, no sense of having my precious disguises robbed.

In recollection, the shiny, self-pitying grandeur of Pink Floyd is among the uneasiest tokens of my teenage tastes. A year or two later I'd give myself to their paranoiac epic *The Wall*, memorizing and debating lyrics in the company of friends my own age. With my pals Joel and Donna I made a pilgrimage to the Nassau Coliseum to see Pink Floyd play the entire double album live from behind a fake wall, which was destroyed by a fake airplane at the show's peak. Then we slumbered in a stoned fever as we rode home, heads lolled on one another's shoulders in seats on the Long Island Rail Road. Yet Pink Floyd was at odds with the musical tastes I'd cultivated otherwise, those more along punk lines, and requiring Talking Heads– or Elvis Costello–style ironies to deflate the sort of hippie pieties which thrived unmistakably beneath Pink Floyd's wounded rage.

Such self-conscious posturing (my own, I mean, not Elvis Costello's) doesn't stand a chance against the kind of helpless love I still feel if I play "Shine on You Crazy Diamond, Part I–V," especially on headphones. My pleasure in the song is in more than the regression cued by my memory of Bob's gentleness with a too-high child. I love the song for what it meant to me after I studied it too—after I learned the story of Pink Floyd's fallen compatriot, Syd Barrett. They were a group that had lost their genius, their spiritual center, and had had to carry on. And, para-doxically, their masterpiece (for that was what I felt "Shine on You Crazy Diamond" to be) was achieved without his help, but in his honor. Syd Barrett wasn't dead, but "Shine on You Crazy Diamond" was memorial art. It suggested that my own wish for a large life—my attempts, even, at greatness—might be compatible with the loss of my mother. I didn't have to fall into ruin to exemplify the cost of losing someone as enor-mous as Judith Lethem, since Pink Floyd had flourished in Barrett's wake. My surviving her death would be in no way Judith's dishonor. I'd only owe her a great song.

Sauve qui peut (la vie) (1980, mom dead)

My father's sometime-girlfriend Hannah and I went out to see the new Godard movie, *Sauve qui peut (la vie)*, or *Every Man for Himself*, at the Quad Theater on Thirteenth Street in Manhattan, on an evening when my father was out with another woman. The film had been widely reviewed as a return to form for Godard, who had for most of the seven-ties renounced the poetry of his sixties style in favor of Marxist agitprop (or anyway that was the received opinion). I'd been watching his sixties films at repertory houses, and loved the ones I (partly) understood: *Breathless, My Life to Live, A Woman Is a Woman, Band of Outsiders, Weekend.* This would be the first time I'd seen a new Godard film at the moment of its release. Hannah was a young painter, sharp and funny, as near my age as my father's. I treasured my friendship with her, even at a time when my anger at my father for surviving my mother was at its very worst, and my treatment of him consisted largely of sullen avoidance.

I didn't understand *Sauve qui peut (la vie)*. I've also never seen it again, so I can't characterize it for you here. I only recall an undertone of political and sexual disappointment that was beyond me. No major shame in that, as Godard can mystify plenty of adults. I did sense the film's beauty, the beauty of a pure cinematic voice that even in its pensiveness evoked grand, unnameable emotions. These days, I see that as Godard's gift, sufficient unto itself: an eroticism of the intellectual life, against which not only the viewer's suppositions but Godard's own ideologies are finally helpless. At fifteen, though, I wasn't at a point where I could trust art which baffled and enraptured me. I needed to feel I'd encompassed it. Perhaps if I'd gone to the movie alone I'd have kidded myself, but in Hannah's company the incompleteness of my response was exposed to me.

We returned to my family's home, an odd move given the situation. There we smoked pot together at my family's kitchen table, a provocation (by both of us) to my absent father, but also an invocation (by me) of my dead mother. It dawned on me that I was being used, a little. Hannah was staking out my dad, seeing if he came home alone, or at all. But that was okay, because I was using Hannah to taunt my father, whether he knew it or not. I wanted to feel I was out on a date with Hannah. The flaw in my game was clear soon enough. As I tired, Hannah grew angry, and my insufficiency as a surrogate became annoying to us both. I wasn't interested enough in this drama because it wasn't about me, so I went to bed.

Something was quietly wrecked. Hannah generously treated me as an equal, so it wasn't her fault that the evening had stripped away part of my disguise, both in terms of Godard and my father. From now on I'd have to go farther from home for my companions, that was the lesson. And *Sauve qui peut (la vie)* became a farewell to Jean-Luc Godard as one of my primary tokens of identification. He'd betrayed me by belonging more to the adults in the full auditorium at the Quad than he had to me as a teenager sitting in mostly empty repertory houses, alone. I quit trying to see all his movies. The sole exception was *Alphaville*, which, with its dystopian noir science-fiction plot, was precisely in my ballpark of satirical paranoia. *Alphaville* was unbudgeable, with Rod Serling's *Twilight Zone*, the Talking Heads album *Fear of Music*, and Kafka, from my deep pantheon. The rest, though, was French to me. In fact, I wouldn't again see a film of Godard's at the moment of its release until I saw *Éloge de l'amour* at the Cannes Film Festival in 2001, with Godard himself in the audience. We gave him a standing ovation. He looked as tired as someone who'd borne the freight of so many expectations for so many years probably ought to look.

The Sorcerer's Apprentice (1978–1986, mom dead)

In the years following my mother's death, when I was fourteen, then fifteen, then sixteen, I forged a series of friendships with grown men, all of them teachers or artists or bohemians or seekers of one kind or another. There was the bon vivant Michael, whose bookshop I haunted until he imported me into his remarkable circle of friends. There was Paul, a Quaker/hippie/army-dropout, whose book of poetry I illustrated. There was Ian, my math teacher in high school, with whom I'd stalk the streets of Greenwich Village after school, engaged in deep talk of existentialist resistance to bourgeois life. More briefly, there was Rolando, a gay black painter and ballet dancer, who gave me a glimpse of New York's homosexual demimonde while leaving me untouched; Mr. Newman, a refined young painter frustrated at being trapped teaching English in a high school for aspiring painters; Mr. Greenberg, my sensitive, bearish sculpture teacher, for whose pleasure I momentarily became a prodigy at marble carving; Steve, a British hippie and world traveler by bicycle, who for a time had been a boyfriend of my mother's, with whom I would stay up all night inflamed by mystical, Gurdjieffian dialogues.

There may even have been others, but it would be a mistake to class any others with these principal three: Michael, Paul, and Ian—call them *the beards.* Each wore a beard, like my father. And it was their beards that made it unmistakable (to my eye) that my friendships were with adults and so that I must therefore be an adult myself, just as it was their beards and my lack of one that must have made it unmistakable (to other eyes) that a kid was hanging out with a grown-up.

My relationships with each of these three, Michael, Paul, and Ian, might have seemed similar to a witness, had there been one. With each of the three I talked about books and movies of the "outsider" variety, smoked pot, complained about the dullness of school and the limited perspective of my peers, and escaped the role of teenager in a house wracked by my mother's death. To each of them, I suppose, I delivered the flattery of my reverence, nicely hidden inside the outlines of genuine friendship. For they were my real friends. No one of these three (nor any of the others) ever hinted at anything paternal in their feeling for me. I would have rejected it irritably, and anyway, they weren't the type. Only in their twenties, Michael, Paul, and Ian were more like older brothers, but we'd never have invoked even that mild analogy. That pretense of equivalence was precious to me, as was the escape from anything to do with family.

For these outward similarities, the flavor of a day in the company of each of these three was violently dissimilar. Michael cultivated a misanthropic air, but drew people to him more compulsively than anyone I've yet known. Trained as an actor, he was an instinctive mimic and scene stealer. In the puppet shows that shared the space of his bookstore, Michael played the "human" character to the puppets: the giant in *Jack and the Beanstalk*, the genie in *Aladdin*, the sorcerer in *The Sorcerer's Apprentice*. His extemporaneous asides in these roles were in the nature of the "adult" part of an entertainment for children, meant to keep parents from growing restive. Yet in rooms full of six- and seven-year-olds and no parents, they seemed aimed solely at me. When the sorcerer turned the apprentice invisible, the spell he spoke aloud would attenuate into lines from Dylan's "Like a Rolling Stone": "You're invisible now, you've got no secrets to conceal, you're a complete unknown, so how does it feel to be on your own?" Michael taught me to delight in the erratic nature of human interaction from within a pose of exasperated worldliness. That he adored people as much as books helped keep me from making too firm a choice between the two, even as he became my idol as a reader and collector.

Paul was more problematic, in that he called to a side of me that remains underdeveloped to this day: the mystical. We even first met one another through my family's involvement in Quakerism. This drab vestige of family connection—our parents had known each other—we strove to leave behind. Our sole use, those days, for our Quaker heritage, was the mysterious Quaker Cemetery in Prospect Park, a private plot grandfathered into the public land, the high gates to which only the Quakers had access. Paul and I got hold of the keys so that we could creep around and take drugs inside the cemetery, where we were fascinated by the chicken heads thrown in by local practitioners of Santeria or voodoo (we weren't sure which). I also wanted to search for Montgomery Clift's grave—Clift's eccentric Quaker mother had had him buried there—but Paul wasn't as interested as I was. He was bored by pop forms. For instance, he knew Philip K. Dick's work, but found it uninteresting except for one novel, *The Three Stigmata of Palmer Eldritch*. In that book Dick had, it seemed to Paul, almost accidentally rattled the doors of perception. Paul's taste was for exoticism, secret knowledge, and he treated not only literature but both sex and drugs as paths to higher realms.

I savored Paul's frank talk of experiences he'd had and I hadn't, and tuned out what stumped me. His book of poetry and memoir, the pages of which I spent six months illustrating, typesetting, and laying-out with an X-acto knife, was similar to our conversation, a collision of things I could and couldn't use. I liked that Paul was a "real" writer. His language was resplendent, but veered into the sort of muzziness that back then always had me guiltily skipping pages in John Fowles or Frank Herbert. I was more literal than Paul. When I brought the finished product of Paul's book into Michael's shop, to insist we display it on a front table, Michael complied, grudgingly. When he glanced inside its pages he spared just a raised eyebrow and slight smile for comment. Michael knew he could devastate his rival wordlessly, not by criticizing the book but by revealing his X-ray capacity to see in my eyes the diffidence I thought I'd hidden.

Ian called to something more atavistic. He earned his misanthropic posture by wholehearted fury and genuine isolation, ornamented brilliantly with provocations, conspiracy theories, and rococo sarcasm. His wild-man math classes were a legend in our high school—he'd drop the lesson and glower, or inform us we were fools to think doing well in math class meant anything in the larger scheme—but I was the kid who followed him home. We'd eat shark's-fin soup at a Chinese-Cuban restaurant on Eighth Avenue, then visit a pool hall or sit on the stoop of a horse-betting hustler pal of his named Bobby.

Talented at whatever he touched, Ian's enthusiasms fell on him like illnesses. He'd spend a month or two writing sonnets or carving stone or mastering the newest theories in particle physics, disdaining as futile what he accomplished—it looked to me—effortlessly. I couldn't keep up, but found my place as a sounding board for both fevers of inspiration and rages of rejection. Fools were everywhere, games were rigged, and striving was pathetic. My challenge was to not point out how our friendship, or Ian's encouragement of my artistic ambitions, or, for that matter, the laughter we shared watching Godard's *Alphaville* at the Bleecker Street Cinema, expressed possibilities of connection that our daily orgy of nihilism denied. Batman might make room for a sidekick, but could Raskolnikov? (Two or three years later, when I dropped out of college, I dragged Ian along with me and another friend on a rambling drive to Boulder, Colorado. His wide-eyed awe at the sight of Kansas cornfields was poignant. He hadn't been out of New York for more than five years.)

Why should a kid who's lost his mother seem to be in search of a replacement father instead? Well, Michael, Paul, and Ian weren't offering me sympathy, at least not a brand of it that cast me as the bereft child I partly was, but didn't wish in any way to be. A grown woman might threaten to do that. A few of my father's girlfriends had, in fact (not Hannah, but others). My sudden need at fourteen was to have evolved out of the primitive contexts of childhood and family, into some sophisticated version of adulthood that disdained bourgeois values. If Michael, Paul, and Ian had one thing in common it was their apparent disinterest in home or hearth. Their values reinforced my notions of a happy bohemian solitude, in which entanglements with women were a siren song of distraction.

This wasn't who I really was, or am now. Nor, necessarily, was it true of my beards. If Michael became the most enduring and versatile of these friendships-as-auditions-for-self, it might be partly because, like me, he wanted a woman near him almost all the time, and maybe even liked their company as friends better than he liked men. But at this moment forgetting my mother seemed to entail forgetting my father, forgetting childhood (I became weirdly blind to the existence of my younger siblings, whose sadness would have mirrored mine back to me), and possibly even forgetting women per se. I threw out most of human life in favor of a handful of unconventional men of the kind I felt I needed to be.

My identification with the figure of the artist was total, yet I couldn't make safe use of the primary totem available to me: my own father. I had to define my distance from Richard Lethem, not only because of the usual reasons but because he was a parent and I refused to be a child. Or perhaps those are the usual reasons, only amplified to a scream. So, in the beards, I found versions of my father that were also problematic enough to make my real father suspicious. Michael, Paul, and Ian seemed dangerous, and not only because they gave me drugs. They must have unnerved him precisely because they resembled him and his friends, yet I was running from our family. If I'd brought the beards home they'd have likely charmed and reassured my father, but if I'd brought them home they'd have lost their charge, so I kept them in fierce quarantine.

But the beards were also a keeping faith with my mother. That all three smoked pot and were enchanting talkers wasn't an accident. In different ways they resembled Judith, and Judith would have liked them. In the period before my mother's worst illness, and her death, each of my parents' lives was populated with members of the opposite sex who fascinated me. My friendships with their various lovers was a projection, a coping mechanism, and a strange richness in my life. So I refused to let it end with Judith's death. In collecting the beards I was providing a supply of imaginary boyfriends for my (now imaginary) mother.

Fear of Music
(1970–present, mom well/sick/dead)

I read all the Narnia books. I read *The Lord of the Rings*. I read every book by Ray Bradbury. I read every book by Raymond Chandler. I reread every book by Raymond Chandler. I read every book by Kurt Vonnegut, including *God Bless You, Mr. Rosewater.* I read every book by Richard Brautigan and Norman Mailer. I kept a complete set of the stories of Guy de Maupassant on the edge of my loft bed, and tried to read one a night until I finished it (I failed). I saw every movie by Stanley Kubrick, except for *Killer's Kiss.* (Later, when I ran the film society at my college, I arranged a screening of *Killer's Kiss* there.) I tried, hopelessly, to see every movie by Jean-Luc Godard and Francois Truffaut, sitting alone at afternoon show-ings of *Tout va bien* and *Jules and Jim* and *The Bride Wore Black* in the repertory houses of Manhattan. I watched *Star Wars* twenty-one times in a single summer, largely alone. I sat alone at the Thalia, on West Ninety-Fifth Street, and watched *2001: A Space Odyssey* three times in one day. Philip K. Dick became my favorite writer, and, spellbound by forty-odd titles listed in the front of a Bantam edition of *Ubik,* I swore to find and read them all, and succeeded. I read *Ubik* itself four or five times. When I was twenty-five I had a miniaturized version of the dust-jacket design of the first edition of *Ubik* tattooed on my left arm. Italo Calvino became my favorite author and I read every book by Italo Calvino. Don DeLillo, same thing. Patricia Highsmith, same thing. Thomas Berger, same thing. I know I've told you some or all of this before.

I played the third album by Talking Heads, called *Fear of Music,* to the point of destroying the vinyl, then replaced it with a new copy. I memo-rized the lyrics, memorized the lyrics to other Talking Heads albums, saw Talking Heads play any chance I got, and when I arrived at college put up a sign in the wing of my dormitory with an arrow pointing down the hall where some Grateful Dead fans lived, reading DEAD HEADS, and an arrow pointing in the direction of the room I shared with my simpatico roommate, reading TALKING HEADS. At the peak, in 1980 or 1981, my identification was so complete that I might have wished to wear the album *Fear of Music* in place of my head so as to be more clearly seen by those around me.

I turned John Ford's *The Searchers* into a ritual and a cause. I bought approximately two hundred Bob Dylan bootlegs. I tried to see every Howard Hawks movie, every Orson Welles movie, every film listed in the *Film Noir Encyclopedia.* For years I calibrated my record collection against the grades in *Christgau's Record Guide: Rock Albums of the*

Seventies, jotting dissenting views in pencil in the margins: Marvin Gaye's *Here, My Dear*, given a B plus by Robert Christgau, got an A from me. *Here, My Dear*, a tormented account of Marvin Gaye's divorce, was a record I was introduced to by someone who thought it was only pathetic and funny—I began defending it from scorn before I'd finished listening to the first side, a response similar to my proprietary defiance on behalf of John Ford's *The Searchers*, which I humiliated myself defending the first time I ever saw it. I regularly fell asleep to a cassette of *Here, My Dear* on Walkman headphones for a few years in college. In my late twenties I lulled myself to sleep to Chet Baker records for a while, and at the peak of my Chet Baker obsession I owned more than fifty Chet Baker CDs, though I was never satisfied because I knew someone who had more than a hundred Chet Baker CDs.

I rarely listen to Chet Baker anymore. I haven't read Vonnegut or Bradbury or Brautigan since I was a child, partly because I'm afraid of what I'll find, partly because they have become inscribed on the interior surface of the eyes through which I read others. I rarely read Don DeLillo, since the binge years when I feverishly read and reread every one of his novels, and when I do now I find myself stirred but confused. The moment DeLillo became in any way fallible to me I experienced a rupture I'm still traumatized by, one which colors my ability to situate him reasonably in my internal landscape of "contemporary letters"—he's either as great as I thought he was when I thought he made all other writing look silly or he's a total disaster. I still think *Barry Lyndon* and *2001: A Space Odyssey* are great films, and *The Killing* a terrific noir, but my notion of Kubrick-as-favorite-director became bewildering after I allowed myself to feel my disappointment in *A Clockwork Orange*, *Lolita*, and *Full Metal Jacket*. Impossible to place in relation to my "grown-up" pantheon of favorites like Kurosawa, Ford, or Cassavetes, Kubrick floats unfixed in my sky, mooning my awestruck teenaged projections back at me.

I couldn't bear to listen to Talking Heads records, even the ones I'd previously revered, after *Naked*, and after David Byrne's early solo records. That subsequent music seemed to my fierce acolyte's heart a betrayal of the idea of Talking Heads, as though David Byrne were an unworthy steward of the art he'd partly created. All their music became poisonously embarrassing to me the moment I realized it wasn't as good as I'd claimed it was (and no band is as good as I'd claimed Talking Heads were in the years I adored them). I suffered other similar, if milder, divorces: from the surrealist painters Magritte and De Chirico, from Jean-Luc Godard, from Brian Eno and David Bowie. These disappointments I managed to modulate: the artists are less like ex-lovers than like friends I keep in my address book but call less often than I used to. It was my splits from Talking Heads and Stanley Kubrick and Don DeLillo that left me as indignant, ashamed, and unmoored as breakups with a girlfriend or wife, wondering who'd failed whom.

Attempting to burrow and disappear into the admiration of certain works of art, I tried to make such deep and pure identification that my integrity as a human self would become optional, a vestige of my relationship to the art. When I first began to write fiction, at eighteen, I conceived that I would write the novels Philip K. Dick hadn't lived to write—that I would continue his work rather than begin my own. Of course, I now think that Philip K. Dick probably lived to write any novel he was capable of writing, as well as a few he wasn't, but at the time it seemed to me tragic that dozens more didn't exist for me to read. That was the sort of tragedy I could allow myself to dwell on, as a teenager: that Philip K. Dick had died, not that my mother had died.

Nightly wearing headphones to memorize Robert Fripp's twenty-one minute guitar solo wasn't finally so different from watching *The Searchers* a dozen times, though one activity was meditative and put me to sleep and the other was busy and made me enraged. In either case, and in dozens of others, I wanted to submit and submerge, even to die a little. I developed a preference, among others, for art that required endurance, that mimicked a galactic endlessness and wore out the nonbelievers. By ignoring my hunger or need to use the bathroom during a three-hour movie by Kubrick or Tarkovsky I'd voted against my body, with its undeniable pangs and griefs, in favor of a self comprised of eyeballs and brain, floating in the void of pure art. If I wasn't afraid of this kind of dissolution I shouldn't be afraid of death, so I'd be an evolutionary step ahead. I downloaded art into myself, but I was also downloading myself out of my family, my body, and my life, onto a bookshelf of Complete Works, or into the ether of music or film.

By trying to export myself into a place that didn't fully exist I asked works of art to bear my expectation that they could be better than life, that they could redeem life. In fact, I believe they are, and do. My life is dedicated to that belief. But still, I asked too much of them: I asked them also to be both safer than life and fuller, a better family. That they couldn't give. At the depths I'd plumb them, so many perfectly sufficient works of art would become thin, anemic. I sucked the juice out of what I loved until I found myself in a desert, sucking rocks for water.

This was especially true of anything that assumed a posture of minimalism or perfectionism, or of chilly, intellectual grandeur. Hence my rage at Stanley Kubrick, Don DeLillo, Jean-Luc Godard, and Talking Heads. The artists who'd seemed to promise the most were the ones who'd created art that stirred me while seeming to absent themselves from emotional risk—so these were the ones capable of failing my needs most violently. When I discovered their imperfections, my own hope of absenting myself from emotional risk seemed imperiled. It was as though in their coolness these artists had sensed my oversized needs and turned away, flinched from what I'd asked them to feel on my behalf. I blamed them, anyway. My declaring a writer or musician or director my favorite, it seemed, contained a kind of suicide pact for my enthusiasm. The disappointment artist was me.

Slow Train Coming
(1979–81, mom dead)

Bob Dylan belonged to my parents, specifically to my mother, who'd even known him very slightly in her days in the folk scene. He was as obvious and omnipresent in our house as the Beatles, but, for a child, nowhere near as alluring as the Beatles. Dylan's songs spoke to me without my paying attention, until my mother's death forced me to parse her record collection for her traces. Then he became crucial in a series of ceremonies that extended also to Nina Simone, Cream, and Carly Simon.

In the same year I befriended Michael, who loved Dylan in the manner he loved his favorite writers, with the same ready disdain for anyone who didn't get it. This was 1979, when Dylan was seen by most liberals to be in dishonor for his born-again Christianity, another sixties illusion smashed. Anyway, for teenagers, Dylan was a part of what punk had supposedly swept away. So listening to Dylan became a token of the perversity of my tastes, something like wearing jodhpurs or earmuffs to school in order to be branded eccentric. I championed him ironically to my peers, who'd shake their heads. In this way I brandished Dylan as a fetish until it was safe for me to love him honestly.

Philip K. Dick was even more of a stealth operator. Amid my fondness for Borges, Eno, *The Twilight Zone*, Orwell's *1984*, Talking Heads, and Kubrick, Dick seemed to be the writer I was waiting for. I liked science fiction but the science fiction I'd located to that point wasn't hip or funny or, mostly, dark enough for my tastes. Dick's profile as King of the Paranoids, which is how I understood it from the jackets of his books, suited me so well that he was almost my official favorite writer before I'd finished a single book. Yet he was no Eno or Kubrick, no David Byrne. Dick's work had a yearning and homely undertow, a self-doubting quality, that made him infinitely richer and more disturbing than I'd assumed. Franz Kafka, another idol who survived my teenage years, was like Dick in concealing personal art within a Trojan horse of paradox and paranoia. As with Dick, I came for the dystopian worldview, and stayed for the self-disclosure.

Oddly enough, Philip K. Dick was also publicly converting to what seemed to me some creepy version of Christianity at that very moment, at the start of the eighties. His spiritual desires, like Dylan's, on one hand repulsed me. Yet in both cases the work that resulted from their religious questioning embedded such elegant uncertainty as to the likelihood of a life's full sustenance in art and ego that my own solipsism was slightly eroded. Before long, too, I'd identified the many points of contact between Philip K. Dick's characters and situations from his own life. The extent and transparency of autobiographical influence made his work as awkwardly confessional as that of Philip Roth, who was exactly the type of writer I thought I'd decided not to admire or become. Dick had urged me past my biases, after it was too late to reject him.

I'd stumbled into each of these loves against my teenage tendencies in hero selection. Rather than arranging yet again to be disappointed by a figure of authority, these guys were like fraternal companions, stumbling through their own ups and downs. Dylan and Dick created bodies of work so contradictory and erratic that they never seemed to have promised me perfection, so they could never disappoint me the way a parent can let down a child who has idolized them. Here were artists who hung themselves emotionally out to dry, who risked rage and self-pity in their work, and were sometimes overwhelmed by those feelings and blew it. As figures of identification they were riskier for me but also, in the long run, more nourishing.

Bob Dylan and Philip K. Dick (and, eventually, others who resembled them in this way) also led me back to my father. For he was of course the artist from whose imperfections, and revealed vulnerabilities, I'd originally flinched. For years I'd chosen against my father by idolizing artists who hid their face behind glossy, impassive surfaces. Yet those figures had proved brittle—inadequate against the untidy barrage of my feelings. They'd refused to meet me where I needed them most, at some emotional substratum down to which I'd excavated and found nobody home. Dylan and Dick, by their own unwillingness to hide their clumsiness and variability, or to protect me from an awareness of the fallible processes behind even their masterpieces, seduced me into sympathy for the artist whose process was, as I grew up, so naked to me. And, needless to say, I had to begin to forgive my father for being human before I could begin to work.

Mr. Natural
(1978–86, mom dead)

In *Broadway Danny Rose*, Woody Allen plays a theatrical agent with a star performer, a singer, who, though married, is carrying on an affair. In order to protect his singer, Allen escorts the mistress around town, allowing them to be mistaken for a couple in order to provide his singer with deniability. When this leads to disaster, and threats of death (the girlfriend is a Mafioso's ex-moll), Allen begs off: "I'm only the beard," he says. "You don't shoot the beard!"

Allen had reintroduced this vivid term, a recent antique. Soon it began cropping up in gossipy magazines, often to describe the heterosexual escort of a secretly gay movie star: *the beard*. A cloak on passions that those who required a beard might be unwilling to discuss or even consider, the beard was itself a figure of power and mystery. For we are revealed not only as our disguises slip or are abandoned but in the nature of the disguises we choose. Pretenses are always either insufficient, overcompensatory, or both. Masks melt into our faces and become impossible to remove precisely at the instant we'd realized they were transparent all along.

Growing up in an artist's family, I seized on comic books and science fiction as a solution to the need to disappoint my father's expectation that I become an artist like himself. These tastes encompassed my real passions: for art that embraced the vernacular vibrancy of pop music and film, and for fusions of imaginative material with the mundane. But they also served as a beard on my own ambition, a cloak on my reverence for the esteemed artifacts of my parents' universe. The cartoonist I settled on lastly, R. Crumb, was of course as late-modernist and literary as they come, a Philip Roth or Robert Coover of comics. His Rabelaisian universe might be off-puttingly grotesque—a bonus, where I was concerned—but his voice, revealed over time, was relentlessly honest, if neurotic. And he obviously adored mundane landscapes and scuffling background characters, which he recorded in scrupulous detail at the margins of his insane inventions. In fact, the juxtaposition of the two provided the depth which separated Crumb from his competitors.

Well before the revealing choice of Crumb, though, I'd been distilling literary pleasure in various Marvel comic books, reading them as inchoate "graphic novels" before the invention of that term. My attention drifted from superheroes at the moment I suspected the majority of their creators were cynical, less interested in their characters' morbid implications than I was. Meanwhile, my favorite writer, Philip K. Dick, draped a junk-culture veil over personal obsessions, then transformed the stuff of his disguise into a higher art than he could recognize. When I learned more about Dick's life I saw I'd instinctively recapitulated his self-exiling, for Dick had wanted nothing more than to be a literary writer. Dick had hardly needed to beard his dangerous liaison with art, though. Literary critics (with their bias) and his publishers (with their garish jacket art) did it for him.

More generally, my obsessiveness about books, songs, and films was a beard on growing up, which I didn't want to catch myself doing. I wanted it behind me while it was ahead of me. This exertion of will (if I'd seen more Godard films than any adult I knew, or read more books by Norman Mailer, then maybe I'd have proved something) was also an act of sensory deprivation, of self-abnegation. The two—will and deprivation—were weirdly compatible. I tried to obliterate my teenage years in movie theaters because my teenage years embarrassed and saddened me. Between double features of French films, between putting one book down and picking up the next, I'd glance at my wristwatch to see if I was in my twenties yet.

And the beards—Michael, Paul, and Ian—were of course a beard for my hazardous love of my parents, in the period when survival had seemed to require numbing myself to my father as a response to the death of my mother. Each was a friend, but also a cover behind which I could engage in fragile experiments in provisional adulthood. The irony may be that for the three of them, single men just in their twenties, mentoring a mother-bereft kid may have been one of the most adult acts of their newly adult lives. Yet to do it at all they had to do it by my terms, which meant pretending we were equals.

So I may have been a beard for the beards as well. By seeming to irresponsibly hang out with a teenager (some would say, seeming to corrupt a teenager), they could dabble in responsibility. I suspect this notion would have startled the beards, precisely because I'd preselected each of them so carefully: not the surrogate-father type. By exchanging good companionship we were able, on both sides, to ignore the central fact in our friendships. Under that cover we were able to simultaneously explore versions of ourselves that would have seemed conflictual had we brought them to light.

In My Room
(1974–present, mom, etc.)

Every room I've lived in since I was given my own room at eleven was lined with, and usually overfull of, books. My employment in bookstores was always continuous with my private hours: shelving and alphabetizing, building shelves, and browsing—in my own collection and others—

in order to understand a small amount about the widest possible number of books. Such numbers of books are constantly acquired that constant culling is necessary; if I slouch in this discipline, the books erupt. I've also bricked myself in with music—vinyl records, then compact discs. My homes have been improbably information-dense, like capsules for survival of nuclear war, or models of the interior of my own skull. That comparison—room as brain—is one I've often reached for in describing the rooms of others, but it began with the suspicion that I'd externalized my own brain, for anyone who cared to look.

The simpler, and perhaps deeper, truth lies in the comparison more obvious to others: that the empires of data storage make up a castle or armor or hermit-crab's shell for my tender self. My exoskeleton of books has peaked in baroque outcroppings and disorderly excess at times of lonely crisis. After my mother died I acquired a friend's vast paperback collection, and the overflow shelving in my room consisted of books balanced on planks unfixed to any wall or support, so that no one apart from me dared lift a book for fear of calamity. Between marriages I've reached such fevers of acquisition that I twice resorted to sleeping on mattresses laid not atop a box spring but a pallet of cartons, the only way to disguise the excess without resorting to storage. Moving books off-site would have felt like putting my arms and legs in hock.

These confessions have begun to bore me, and I only want to make a few more. The adult life I've made—getting paid, reader, to tell you these things—bears a suspicious resemblance to the rooms themselves. My prose is a magpie's, even when not larded with cultural name-dropping, as have been my last two novels, as is this piece of no-longer-particularly-veiled memoir. Perhaps anyone's writing is ultimately bricolage, a welter of borrowings. But of the writers I know, I've been the most eager to point out my influences, to spoil the illusion of originality by elucidating my fiction's resemblance to my book collection. I want it both ways, of course. At fifteen I wished to be like Michael, who drew admirers into a bookstore he seemed to be exhibiting almost grudgingly, as a private museum of his interests. My rooms might have been armor, a disguise or beard, but I wanted millions of admirers to peek inside and see me there, and when they did I wished for them to revere and pity me at once. The contradiction in this wish tormented me, so I ignored it. Then I became a writer and it began to sustain me. I may still be trying to make it come true now, by working here to arouse your pity and reverence for the child I was.

The Collected Works of Judith Lethem
(1978–present, blah blah blah)

My mother, because of her verbal flair, and her passion for books, was taken or mistaken by her friends as a writer-to-be. She sometimes spoke of writing, but I doubt she ever tried. Pregnant at twenty-one, and a mother of three by the time she, at thirty-two, began to die, she never had much chance. It is impossible to know whether she would have made anything of the chance if she had.

Her gift to me on my fourteenth birthday, the last while she was alive, was a manual typewriter. The summer after her death, when I was fifteen, I wrote a 125-page "novel" with the manual typewriter, mostly on torn-out, blue-lined notebook paper. In that same year I typed poems, of a fragmentary and impulsive sort. Truthfully, they more resembled song lyrics, since I wasn't a reader of poems then. I recall one which spoke of my mother and the possibility of her writing. "You can't write when you're sick in bed," was its much-repeated chorus; I don't remember more. This poem was on one hand sympathetic. I knew, at least consciously, that my mother's illness was involuntary. So I offered forgiveness: she couldn't be blamed for not having written. Yet it was also an admonitory poem—really, admonitory to myself.

Since then, I've been in a hurry. Writing is another meditation that's also a frantic compensation. As if wearing headphones, I'm putting some of myself to sleep, rushing to the end of my days: there's a death wish in reducing life to watching one's fingers twitch on the alphabet. I'm as pathetic as that kid watching double features alone, but also as vain. Writing's an aggression on the world of books, one reader's bullying attempt to make himself known to others like him. My heroes Greene, Dick, and Highsmith left many dozens of novels; I'm on pace to write at best ten or twelve of the things. Still, I'm building my shelf. Like the comedian Steven Wright, who said "I keep my seashell collection scattered on the beaches of the world," my teenage room is still expanding, like the universe itself. If writing's a beard on loss, then, like some character drawn by Dr. Seuss, I live in my own beard.

What's one supposed to say when the mask comes off? Is there an etiquette I'm breaking with? John Lennon recorded a song, for his first album after the breakup of the Beatles (what a grand beard *that* was, art and companionship blended together, and the worshiping world at his feet!), called "My Mummy's Dead." I suppose this is my version of that song. I sing it now in order to quit singing it. Mine has been a paltry beard anyway, the peach-fuzzy kind a fifteen-year-old grows, so you still see the childish face beneath. Each of my novels, antic as they may sometimes be, is fueled by loss. I find myself speaking about my mother's death everywhere I go in this world.

A critic once said that every serious poem's true subject, whether obvious or not, is death. Yet to write more than one poem you'd better find a way to forget you heard that. If life itself is, after all, only a beard for death, couldn't the reverse be true as well?

ALSO BY JONATHAN LETHEM

AS SHE CLIMBED ACROSS THE TABLE
Alice, a particle physicist, has left her boyfriend, Philip, for Lack, a void she and her colleagues have created. To Philip, Lack is an unbeatable rival, for how can he win Alice back from something that has no flaws—because it has no qualities.

Fiction/0-375-70012-9

THE FORTRESS OF SOLITUDE
Dylan Ebdus and Mingus Rude grow up motherless in downtown Brooklyn in the 1970s. As Lethem follows their biracial friendship, he creates a canvas of race and class, superheroes, gentrification, funk, hip-hop, graffiti-tagging, loyalty, and memory.

Fiction/0-375-72488-5

GIRL IN LANDSCAPE
Thirteen-year-old Pella Marsh emigrates with her family to the Planet of the Archbuilders. These enigmatic aborigines baffle and frighten their human visitors and the spikily independent Pella becomes an uneasy envoy between two species.

Fiction/0-375-70391-8

MEN AND CARTOONS
A boozy ex-military captain searches for his runaway son, an aging superhero settles into academia, and a professional "dystopianist" receives a visit from a suicidal sheep. This visionary collection of eleven stories features two stories not published in its hardcover edition, "This Shape We're In" and "Interview with the Crab."

Fiction/Short Stories/1-4000-7680-3

MOTHERLESS BROOKLYN
Lionel Essrog, an orphan whose Tourettic impulses drive him to rip apart language, works for small-time mobster Frank Minna. When Frank is fatally stabbed, Lionel must untangle the threads of the case while trying to keep words straight in his head.

Fiction/0-375-72483-4

The Vintage Book of Amnesia, 0-375-70661-5

Available at your local bookstore, or call toll-free to order:
1-800-793-2665 (credit cards only).